INDIGENOUS SOVEREIGNTY AND
THE BEING OF THE OCCUPIER

TRANSMISSION

Transmission denotes the transfer of information, objects or forces from one place to another, from one person to another. Transmission implies urgency, even emergency: a line humming, an alarm sounding, a messenger bearing news. Through Transmission interventions are supported, and opinions overturned. Transmission republishes classic works in philosophy, as it publishes works that re-examine classical philosophical thought. Transmission is the name for what takes place.

INDIGENOUS SOVEREIGNTY AND THE BEING OF THE OCCUPIER

MANIFESTO FOR A WHITE AUSTRALIAN PHILOSOPHY OF ORIGINS

Toula Nicolacopoulos
George Vassilacopoulos

re.press Melbourne 2014

re.press

PO Box 40, Prahran, 3181, Melbourne, Australia
http://www.re-press.org

© T. Nicolacopoulos & G. Vassilacopoulos 2014
The moral rights of the authors have been asserted

This work is 'Open Access', published under a creative commons license which
means that you are free to copy, distribute, display, and perform the work
as long as you clearly attribute the work to the authors, that you do not use
this work for any commercial gain in any form whatsoever and that you in
no way alter, transform or build on the work outside of its use in normal
academic scholarship without express permission of the author (or their
executors) *and* the publisher of this volume. For any reuse or distribution,
you must make clear to others the license terms of this work. For more
information see the details of the creative commons licence at this website:
http://creativecommons.org/licenses/by-nc-sa/3.0/

National Library of Australia Cataloguing-in-Publication entry

Nicolacopoulos, Toula, author.

Indigenous sovereignty and the being of the occupier :
manifesto for a white Australian philosophy of origins /
Toula Nicolacopoulos and George Vassilacopoulos.

ISBN: 9780980819717 (paperback)

Series: Transmission.

Group identity--Australia.
National characteristics, Australian.
Citizenship--Australia.
Australia--Social conditions.
Australia--Emigration and immigration--Social aspects.

Other Authors/Contributors: Vassilacopoulos, George, author.

303.40994

Designed and Typeset by A&R

This book is produced sustainably using plantation timber, and printed in
the destination market reducing wastage and excess transport.

CONTENTS

1. Introduction: The Call for a Manifesto   9
2. The Need for a White Australian Philosophical Historiography   15
3. The 'Hypothetical Nation' as Being Without Sovereignty   25
4. A Genealogy of the West as the Ontological Project of the Gathering-We   35
5. Ontological Sovereignty and the Hope of a White Australian Philosophy of Origins   47
6. The World-Making Significance of Property Ownership in Western Modernity   51
7. Sovereign Being and the Enactment of Property Ownership   57
8. The Onto-Pathology of White Australian Subjectivity   61
9. Racist Epistemologies of a Collective Criminal Will   71
10. The Perpetual-Foreigner-Within as an Epistemological Construction   83
11. The Migrant as White-Non-White and White-But-Not-White-Enough   91
12. Three Images of the Foreigner-Within: Subversive, Compliant, Submissive   95
13. The Imperative of the Indigenous - White Australian Encounter   103

References   107

To Aileen Moreton-Robinson for her generosity of spirit

Indigenous people cannot forget the nature of migrancy and position all non-Indigenous people as migrants and diasporic. Our ontological relationship to land, the ways that country is constitutive of us, and therefore the inalienable nature of our relationship to land, marks a radical, indeed incommensurable, difference between us and the non-Indigenous. This ontological relation to land constitutes a subject position that we do not share, and which cannot be shared, with the postcolonial subject whose sense of belonging in this place is tied to migrancy.

Aileen Moreton-Robinson[1]

---

1. Aileen Moreton-Robinson, 'I Still Call Australia Home: Indigenous Belonging and Place in a White Postcolonising Society', in Sara Ahmed, Claudia Cataneda, Ann Marie Fortier and Mimi Shellyey (eds.), *Uprootings/Regroupings: Questions of Postcoloniality, Home and Place,* London and New York, Berg, 2003, pp. 23-40.

1. INTRODUCTION: THE CALL FOR A MANIFESTO

> *A spectre is haunting white Australia, the spectre of Indigenous sovereignty. All the powers of old Australia have entered into a holy alliance to exorcise this spectre: politicians and judges, academics and media proprietors, businesspeople and church leaders.*

To state the obvious and to render something obvious by stating it, this is the aim of a manifesto. To produce a manifesto is to articulate a common sense of fundamentals and thus to suggest a way of becoming visible from within them. It is an exercise in naming oneself or, rather, in uttering one's being: I am free, I am just, I belong here, I am sorry, I love you, I will die for you. It is therefore a philosophical exercise, an account of origins, of where one comes from. Only by giving such an account does one become visible.

There are many ways of appearing, many ways of being. One may appear by emerging from within one's own place of dwelling, as when one comes out of one's home to greet a foreigner. One may also appear from within the space of another's sovereign being, as when history has thrown one into a foreign place to become a migrant or refugee. Or, one may emerge from within the place one has claimed by force, by dispossessing the genuine owner. *Place* is fundamental to all these ways of presenting one's being as one's own but equally so is the *willingness to dwell* in such a place, whether as one's own or with the acknowledgement that it belongs to another.

At least three ways of being then: sovereign being, foreigner being and the being of the occupier. Homer's *Odyssey* offers powerful illustrations of the first two ways of being and of their mutual dependence:

> All these things are performed for him, our honored guest,
> The royal send-off here and gifts we give in love,
> Treat your guest and suppliant like a brother,
> Anyone with a touch of sense knows that.
> So, don't be crafty now, my friend, don't hide
> The truth I'm after. Fair is fair, speak out!
> Come, tell us the name they call you at home,
> [...]
> And tell me your land, your people, your city too,
> [...]
> But come my friend,
> Tell us your own story now and tell it truly.[1]

Here, the sovereign emerges from within the space of his sovereign being in the very act of welcoming and offering hospitality to the foreigner. The foreigner is in turn called upon to give a frank account of himself only after he has been fully welcomed. As regards the third manner of being, that of the occupier, European history is saturated with its myriad manifestations. We might even read this history as the movement in time of just the sort of being that unjustly dwells in foreign places the world over.

White Australia is a case in point. Speaking about the naming of the Western Victorian mountain ranges, Tony Birch writes,

> To name spaces is to 'name histories' [...] and also to create them. The process is accepted as natural, representing a 'given' that this country belongs to and is a white Australia. But this sense of security evaporates when the hidden history of colonial domination and Indigenous subordination is challenged by an attempt to alter the names of spaces.[2]

---

1. Nestor, King of Pylos, addresses Telemachus, son of Odysseus, who arrives in Pylos in search of news of his father's whereabouts. Homer, *The Odyssey*, trans. Robert Fagles, New York, Penguin, 1996, pp. 208-9.

2. Tony Birch, 'Nothing has Changed: The Making and Unmaking of

Is there a need for a manifesto for white Australia? Is there a need for white Australians to name, not the spaces we inhabit but our own being in relation to them? There is indeed such a need precisely because our history has been, and still is being, shaped by a certain command: 'name yourself', 'come out of your hiding and present yourself', 'give a truthful account of your own story'.

Clearly, the force of the command derives from the fact that it is addressed directly and unconditionally to our very being. But who commands with such absolute authority that we dare not refrain from listening? The source of the command is the sovereign being of the Indigenous peoples. In the words of Steve Larkin,

> Within the Australian polity, the notion of Indigenous people as a sovereign people derives from the position that Indigenous people have never ceded their land and continue to feel separate, both in terms of identity and in the ways they are treated differently from other Australians.[3]

This sovereign being perpetually commands white Australians to name our selves as the bearers of the being of an occupier of foreign land. For Irene Watson,

> It is in thinking through how to engage with Aboriginal sovereignties that Australian society [...] becomes 'stuck', where the ground of 'impossibility' lies, but it is this ground 'exactly' where our thinking should begin.[4]

So in their capacity as the source of the command, the Indigenous peoples present to white Australia as belonging to their sovereign world.

Koorie Culture', in Michelle Grossman (ed.), *Blacklines: Contemporary Critical Writing by Indigenous Australians*, Melbourne, Melbourne University Press, 2003, pp. 145-158 at p. 150.

3. Steve Larkin, 'Locating Indigenous Sovereignty: Race and Research in Indigenous Health Policy-making', in Aileen Moreton-Robinson (ed.), *Sovereign Subjects: Indigenous Sovereignty Matters*, NSW Australia, Allen and Unwin, 2007, pp. 168-178 at p. 168.

4. Irene Watson, 'Settled and Unsettled Spaces: Are We free to Roam?', in Aileen Moreton-Robinson (ed.), *Sovereign Subjects: Indigenous Sovereignty Matters*, NSW Australia, Allen and Unwin, 2007, pp. 15-32 at p. 25.

Yet unlike the Homeric figure whose encounter with the foreigner is indeed an encounter with the unfamiliar, the Indigenous peoples of Australia already live out a certain response to the call for a truthful account of the event of European occupation. As Aileen Moreton-Robinson observes:

> colonial experiences have meant Indigenous people have been among the nation's most conscientious students of whiteness and racialisation.[5]

At the same time, in rendering white Australians as the addressees of the command, the command in turn transforms the addressees into bearers of a whole world, the world of the occupier. The command thus becomes *the meeting place* of two worlds and their corresponding accounts of their origins. This is how we understand Fiona Nicoll's representation of 'the ground of Indigenous sovereignty as the place where all Australians come into relationship'.[6]

To name ourselves as-a-world and through such naming to accept full responsibility for our world, this is the challenge. Accordingly, the command at once identifies and commands those who belong to the collective of white Australians to give an account of our origins, of the *topos* we come from and to which we return whenever we confront the fundamentals of our being as an occupier. In calling upon us to utter our being as a collective, the command demands from us that we function through such uttering as the *atopos topos* of dwelling for the collective to which each one of us belongs. In this sense, it demands from us that we be,

---

5. Aileen Moreton-Robinson, 'Whiteness, Epistemology and Indigenous Representation' in Aileen Moreton-Robinson (ed.), *Whitening Race: Essays in Social and Cultural Criticism*, Canberra, Aboriginal Studies Press, 2004, pp. 75-88 at p. 85.

6. Fiona Nicoll, 'De-facing *Terra Nullius* and Facing the Public Secret of Indigenous Sovereignty in Australia' *borderlands e-Journal*, vol.1, no.2, 2002, http://www.borderlands.net.au/vol1no2_2002/nicoll_defacing.html . See also Fiona Nicoll, 'Reconciliation in and out of Perspective: White Knowing, Seeing, Curating and Being at Home in and against Indigenous Sovereignty', in Aileen Moreton-Robinson (ed.), *Whitening Race: Essays in Social and Cultural Criticism*, Canberra, Aboriginal Studies Press, 2004, pp. 17-31.

philosophically. This is possible only in so far as Indigenous sovereign being already embraces the white Australian with a power that one cannot hope to resist without at the same time shattering one's ontological foundations. In the present context to allow oneself to be embraced by that which, as a matter of fact, already embraces one is to liberate oneself from the concealment of one's being as the bearer of the world of the occupier. This then is the challenge that Indigenous sovereign being poses to white Australia.

In a scene from *Traveling Players,* a film in which Theo Angelopoulos engages with the history of modern Greece, just moments before he is shot a Greek patriot poses a question to the German execution squad confronting him: 'I come from [... here]. Where do you come from?' The film is a profound meditation on issues of belonging, identity and occupation, of resistance, vision, sacrifice and betrayal. The patriot's question is never answered. Did the soldiers hear it? Did they understand it? Perhaps in and through this artistically articulated life and death encounter we can discern the contours of the fate of the German occupier or, for that matter, of the modern Westerner as occupier. Unable to answer the question, the German commander gives the order to shoot and thereby annihilates the historical opportunity for catharsis and wisdom. A frank response to the calling that the question is would undoubtedly shatter the occupier's ontological foundations. His being would have been destroyed by an unbearable crisis of self-doubt. Moreover, to accept the absolute ethical force of the uttering of the statement 'I come from here' would have meant the annihilation of the ideological horizons of his proud empire. Yet, such a crisis would also constitute the origin of a freedom. This is the freedom to become free that is made possible by liberation from the very power and the mind-set that affirm one's being as an occupier in the first place.

True heirs to this tradition of power and self-denial, white Australians are today still refusing to become free. In our two centuries-long refusal to hear the words—'I come from here. Where do you come from?'—that the sovereign being of the Indigenous peoples poses to us, we have taken the Western occupier's mentality to a new, possibly ultimate, level. Unable to retreat from the land we have occupied since 1788, and lacking the courage unconditionally to surrender power to the Indigenous peoples, white Australia has become ontologically disturbed. Suffering what we describe as 'onto-pathology', white Australia has become dependent upon 'the perpetual-foreigners-within', those migrants in relation to whom the so-called 'old Australians' assert their imagined difference. For the dominant white Australian, freedom and a sense of belonging do not derive from rightful dwelling in this land but from the affirmation of the power to receive and to manage the perpetual-foreigners-within, that is, the Asians, the Southern European migrants, the Middle Eastern refugees, or the Muslims. In an act of Nietzchean resentment, white Australia has cultivated a slave morality grounded in a negative self-affirmation.[7] Instead of the claim, 'I come from here. You are not like me, therefore you do not belong', the dominant white Australian asserts: 'you do not come from here. I am not like you, therefore I *do* belong'. Might the depth of this self-denial manifest dramatically, not in any failure to embrace a more positive moral discourse but, in the fact that white Australia has yet to produce a philosophy and a history to address precisely that which is fundamental to its existence, namely our being as occupier?

---

7. For discussion of this element of Nietzsche's notion of 'slave morality' see Gilles Deleuze, *Nietzsche and Philosophy*, trans. Hugh Tomlinson, New York, Columbia University Press, 1983, pp. 119-122.

2. THE NEED FOR A WHITE AUSTRALIAN PHILOSOPHICAL HISTORIOGRAPHY

If, as Hegel teaches, philosophy is its era understood in thought, white Australia has yet to produce its own philosophy and white Australians have yet to dwell in this land philosophically. Here 'philosophy' refers to those concepts that spring from the conditions determining one's history and instituted being and which in turn give conceptual shape to those conditions and thereby render them an object of engagement for political consciousness. So, for example, the nationhood of a nation always relates to philosophical encounters with history, that is, encounters involving the fundamentals of a people's being as an historical agent interested in its ontological and ethical integrity, in its freedom and responsibility. It is in this sense that philosophy offers an account of origins, a genealogy of where one comes from. Moreover, it performs the role, to some degree, of educator of the nation in so far as it engages in the practice of (re)situating the self-understandings of the collective present within the context of collective origins.

The absence of a self-consciously white Australian philosophy is implied by the fact that we have yet to formulate an answer to the question 'where do you come from?' that the uncompromising presence of Indigenous sovereign being poses to us. It is this question that commands white Australians to respond by situating ourselves philosophically in relation to our origins. To do so would be to claim our origins as the only thing that is *our very own*. Yet, our unwillingness to take up this radical challenge has itself been elevated to the *topos* of dwelling that we call home. In many respects we have yet to identify the question. Without proper acknowledgement of the question and without developing the appropriate philosophical concepts both theoretically and politically, we will never be in a position to enter history as self-determining agents capable of creating a vision of presence and ontological integrity for ourselves. The ancient Greeks were concerned with *axioprepeia*—the condition of being worthy of what is proper. White Australians need a philosophy to show us what is proper and an historically informed politics to teach us how to be worthy of what is proper.

From this vantage point, the philosophies and the histories of white Australia to date read more like (desperate) attempts to shield us from our history, a history focused on the annihilation of Indigenous sovereign being. In the words of Tony Birch,

> The victors' histories falsely parade as the history of Australia. [...] Europeans have either denied the Indigenous peoples presence, or have completely devalued our cultures. These hegemonic histories take possession of others' histories and silence them, or manipulate and 'deform' them.[8]

Michael Dodson explains,

> Indigenous peoples have rarely come into a genuine relationship with non-Indigenous peoples, because a relationship requires two, not just one and its mirror. Our subjectivities, our aspirations, our ways of seeing and our languages have largely been excluded from the equation, as the colonizing culture plays with itself. It is as if we have been ushered onto a stage to play a drama where the parts have already been written. Choose from the part of the ancient noble spirit, the lost soul estranged from her true nature, or the aggressive drunkard, alternately sucking and living off the system. No other parts are available for 'real Aborigines'.[9]

---

8. Tony Birch, 'Nothing has Changed', p. 152.
9. Michael Dodson, 'The End in the Beginning: Re(de)fining

If we reflect on white Australia as a product of the history-making that manifests the white nation's occupier being *as a whole* the essentials of a short history become visible in terms of two distinct targets for the annihilation of Indigenous sovereign being, namely *the bearer of the question* of our true origins as well as *the question* itself.

But anyone who would take seriously the claim that white Australia is in urgent need of a new way of reflecting upon its own origins must initially confront an apparent rebuttal. One might object that, at least in more recent decades, historians have been addressing precisely this question of Australia's national origins. Is it not the case that the great volumes academic historians have produced now supply the answers that serve to inform the collective conscience of the white nation? Just as historical research practices had previously been crucial for perpetuating a kind of collective amnesia, the latter half of the twentieth century saw a reflective turn in the way we perceive ourselves, and this has given rise to historical research that is the driving force behind clearly cathartic aspirations.[10] According to the 'evidence' that white historians have been unearthing, the nation's founding act admittedly involved racist violence through which the Indigenous peoples were unjustifiably denied their status and rights as sovereign peoples. This mediating act of dispossession via the misrepresentation of the land as *terra nullius* created the space for the emergence of white Australia. But what more is there to be said and what could possibly be the point of *philosophical* reflection given the weight of the empirical evidence, which ultimately led the High Court

---

Aboriginality', in Michelle Grossman (ed.), *Blacklines: Contemporary Critical Writing by Indigenous Australians*, Melbourne, Melbourne University Press, 2003, pp. 25-42 at p. 37.

10. See, for example, Bain Attwood, *The Making of the Aborigines,* Sydney, Allen & Unwin, 1989. John Arnold and Bain Attwood (eds.), *Power, Knowledge and Aborigines*, Melbourne, La Trobe University Press in association with the National Centre for Australian Studies, Monash University, 1992. Bain Attwood, *Telling the Truth about Aboriginal History*, Sydney, Allen & Unwin, 2005.

of Australia to overturn the doctrine of *terra nullius*?[11]

Far from seeking to annihilate Indigenous sovereignty by targeting both the question of origins and its bearer, on this view, white historians do not need to formulate a 'philosophy of origins' since, through the turn of their academic gaze towards our historical shadow, the black shadow of the white nation, they have already dramatically and vividly given an account of those origins. They have told us that white Australians have never seen the blood of the sacrifice of their national heroes because this blood never mixed with the Australian earth. The only blood they have seen return to the earth from which it was drawn was the blood of the black patriot shot by the white invader. If so, then any failure on the part of the white *philosopher* to 'discover' history, and the related desire to allow history to speak through philosophy, would appear to have been mitigated by the achievements of the *historian* who has emerged as the ultimate truth bearer of the white nation. In a similar vein today's anthropologist aspires to address precisely the relationality of contexts that was denied by earlier representations of Aboriginal people.[12] The achievements of the white historian and anthropologist thus compare only to the silence of the philosopher, a silence that has only just begun to be broken.[13]

And yet, we are suggesting that white historiography and anthropology have not been able to engage the very heart of white Australian being, the being of the occupier. This latter is the ultimate determining condition of the white nation and the failure to engage it amounts to a failure to produce a

---

11. *Mabo v the State of Queesnland*, (No.2) (1992) 175 CLR 1.

12. See, for example, Tess Lea, Emma Kowal and Gillian Cowlishaw (eds.), *Moving Anthropology: Critical Indigenous Studies*, Northern Territory, Australia, Charles Darwin University Press, 2006. For critical discussion of this point see Aileen Moreton-Robinson, 'How White Possession Moves: After the Word', in T. Lea, E. Kowal and G. Cowlishaw (eds.), *Moving Anthropology: Critical Indigenous Studies*, Northern Territory, Australia, Charles Darwin University Press, 2006, pp. at p. 219.

13. Genevieve Lloyd, 'No one's Land; Australia and the Philosophical Imagination', *Hypatia*, vol.15, no.2, 2000, pp. 26-39. See also the articles in the 'Special Issue on Indigenous Rights', *Australasian Journal of Philosophy*, vol.78, no.3, 2000.

history that springs from the depths of the white Australian ontology. It is in this sense that white historiography has yet to become sufficiently philosophical. On what might we base this observation? Although accounts of Indigenous dispossession may vary significantly, the practice of writing them into an *Australian* history reveals an unacknowledged underlying commitment amongst white Australian historians. This is a commitment to the view that white Australia would have been *essentially* the same had the European conquerors actually discovered an unoccupied continent. The origins and the development of the white Australian nation are typically represented as being essentially a matter between the European 'settlers' and the land that was slowly 'civilized' and transformed into an integral part of European world history. From the perspective of this deeply rooted commitment from which springs our fundamental self-conception, the real decisive moment that shaped the ontology of the white collective was the fall of the first eucalyptus to the axe of the white settler and not the death of the first Indigenous Australian at the hands of the white invader. Differences aside, the history books generally affirm the conviction that the white Australians are *essentially* settlers and only *accidentally* occupiers.

Could the nation-building processes of a nation in self-denial have proceeded otherwise? White Australians generally live our history as informed by a certain widespread and very deeply held, if unacknowledged, view. This is the view that we have no reason to think that we would have been a dramatically different people—with different institutions and priorities and different ways of developing our 'young and free' nation—were the Indigenous peoples of Australia non-existent. The vastness of the land would have been the same just as our efforts to tame the land would have been the same. Our heroic explorers would have been no less heroic. Our convict past, with all its associated brutality, would still have been glorified as the humble beginnings of a greatly successful social experiment. Nothing would need to have been different about our feelings for

Australia's British heritage, our liberal institutions or even our racism and our attitudes towards the non-British migrants. The list can go on.

Nevertheless, the proof of our claim lies in those history writing practices of the white nation that respond sympathetically to the reality of Indigenous dispossession, for they serve as the most vivid illustrations of the 'secret' we are not even whispering to our selves. They are typically written in a way that enables the reader of the history of white Australia to miss nothing of significance in the development of their narrative were he or she to skip the pages that refer to Australia's Aboriginal history. Even the references to our racism need not be dramatically modified given that they typically represent the racism towards Indigenous Australians as but one expression of a racist appetite that has found many ways of satisfying itself. Even when exposing the falsity of the doctrine of *terra nullius*, the writing of the white nation proceeds through the development of narratives that unfold *as if* the land might indeed have been unoccupied. This is the mechanism by which the white historian, in cooperation with judges, lawyers and politicians, continues to be an integral part of the processes of annihilating the question that Indigenous sovereign being poses.

Given these circumstances, how might white Australia proceed to 'tell its story truly'? Rather than including the history of the Aborigines as part of *our* history, perhaps the answer to our question is to be found in a reversal of this relation. In the words of Tony Birch,

> Where might we 'progress' to, then, if we are to collectively produce a future more substantive that the deception offered at present? [...] Non-Indigenous Australia needs to reassess its place within an Indigenous nation, including a willingness to accede to the principles of Indigenous sovereignty, amongst which are a respect for Indigenous knowledge systems and the historical landscapes from which they were created.[14]

---

14. Tony Birch, 'The Invisible Fire: Indigenous Sovereignty, History and Responsibility', in Aileen Moreton-Robinson (ed.), *Sovereign Subjects: Indigenous Sovereignty Matters*, NSW Australia, Allen and Unwin, 2007, pp.

We would be in a better position to come to terms with the whole of our being as occupiers were we to locate ourselves within the history of the Indigenous peoples, appreciating it as the all-encompassing horizon within which our own story might come to life. But, to locate white Australian being within the history of the Indigenous peoples cannot simply be a matter of the whites acknowledging our own Aboriginality, as some have proposed.[15] Nor can it be a matter of extending to Indigenous Australian authors (some semblance of) the white authorial power thus enabling them to generate their own accounts of the facts alongside others. For, as Tracey Bunda explains,

> Indigenous people write from their sovereign positions as owners of their land. [...] Our sovereignty is embodied and is tied to particular tracts of country, thus our bodies signify ownership and we perform sovereign acts in our everyday living. Writing by Indigenous people is thus a sovereign act.[16]

Precisely because Australian history happens on the collective body of the Indigenous peoples as a primordial and ongoing event of occupation, to locate ourselves within the history of this place is primordially to become involved in an ontological transformation. Such a transformation must involve a process that recognizes the resisting being of the occupied, unconditionally. Gary Foley writes,

> From the very beginning Indigenous peoples resisted and opposed the invasion and occupation of their lands. Since the 1860s, as the Aboriginal peoples in regional areas of southeastern Australia experienced the spread of the white invasion and forcible occupation of their homelands, there can be said to have been significant resistance, both passive and active.[17]

105-117 at p. 114.

15. See, for example, Peter Read, 'A Haunted land no Longer? Changing Relationships to a Spiritualised Australia', *Australian Book Review*, no. 265, 2004, pp. 29-34.

16. Tracey Bunda, 'The Sovereign Aboriginal Woman', in Aileen Moreton-Robinson (ed.), *Sovereign Subjects: Indigenous Sovereignty Matters*, NSW Australia, Allen and Unwin, 2007, pp. 75-85 at p.75.

17. Gary Foley, 'The Australian Labor Party and the Native Title Act', in

Aileen Moreton-Robinson explains,

> Indigenous people have spent a long time looking at and resisting the powerful. We have become extremely knowledgeable about white Australia in ways that are unknown to most white 'settlers'. Our social worlds are imbued with meaning grounded in knowledges of different realities. In our communities, through the vehicle of oral history, social memory is developed, reproduced, changed and maintained. The message of resistance is embedded in local histories and is performed in embodied daily practices.[18]

The naming of white Australian being as that of the occupier thus depends upon this resisting being. In other words, in so far as it already provides the answer to the question 'where do you come from?' Indigenous resistance, struggle and survival perpetually expose white Australia to what is fundamental to our ontology, our occupier being. From this perspective, to accept our being for what it is, the being of the occupier, is ultimately to involve ourselves in an ontological act of unconditional surrender to (the word of) the sovereign Indigenous peoples of Australia. This is why it is the other who inevitably writes us into a collective history.

The failure on our part to surrender unconditionally also explains why white Australia has yet to produce its true historian in as much as it has failed to produce its own philosopher. In other words, the historian of the white nation has yet to dwell on this land philosophically. Whereas reflection without attentiveness to its ontology is at best busy recruiting facts and arguing over their authenticity, the first true act of the historian-cum-philosopher would be to open the door of history thus enabling us to become visionary, not as the great narrator of our true past, but in

---

Aileen Moreton-Robinson (ed.), *Sovereign Subjects: Indigenous Sovereignty Matters*, NSW Australia, Allen and Unwin, 2007, pp. 118-139 at p. 121.

18. Aileen Moreton-Robinson, 'Introduction: Resistance, Recovery and Revitalization' in Michelle Grossman (ed.), *Blacklines: Contemporary Critical Writing by Indigenous Australians*, Melbourne, Melbourne University Press, 2003, pp. 127-131 at p. 127.

refusing to assert authorial power, to write the history, to record the facts, of the white nation. To utter the words, 'I refuse', to smash the pen and tear up the paper, would be to release us from 'the discovery of historical facts' and to throw us into the very fact of history. Whilst it is true, in a trivially obvious manner, that history is nothing without facts, it is also true, and true in a primordial sense, that facts are dead without the opening that history offers. To the *thanatology* of facts that the white historian typically practices we must counter-pose the living force of history, the defiant being of the occupied that frames these facts and gives them their significance.

If we are right about this, then the challenge for white Australian historiography cannot be *to write* but *to be written*, to-be-as-written, by the infinite other of and incommensurably different from the migrant. For our part, as surrendered, we may only listen, attempt to survive the telling of the story, and grow free through such listening. On this scenario, the historian's great refusal to assert historiographical power would have the effect of violently and dramatically introducing into the consciousness of white Australia the awareness that the history of the occupier *as such,* the history of a self-inflicted loss of being and agency, can only be comprehensively told from the position of the occupied who already knows us more deeply and whose knowledge completely and unconditionally penetrates our being as a whole. Our real concern then cannot simply be with the truth born of the historical and cultural facts that the white historian and anthropologist are positioned to reveal to us but with the Indigenous bearer of the truth of our collective history.

In the words of Lester-Iribanna Rigney,

> The concepts of freedom and liberation from neo-colonialism cannot be discussed meaningfully outside the practice of Indigenous intellectual sovereignty. Indigenous intellectual sovereignty means moving toward a cultural criticism that is embedded in the Indigenous Australian experience, and that is influenced by the intellectual work we do as scholars for

the social, political, economic and cultural struggle of Indigenous Australians.[19]

If, as we maintain, the true historians of the white nation-state are the Indigenous peoples, precisely because the ontology of this nation-state is violently shaped on and through their collective body, then the concern of the white Australian cannot be other than philosophical. For only a *philosophical* engagement has the potential to reveal the very meaning of unconditional surrender and with this the meaning and value of listening. Just as our historiographical powers might lead us to the wisdom of silence, so too in our capacity to philosophize we might eventually produce words that authentically belong to the white nation. The historian's silence alongside the political vision of unconditional surrender offer the hope of freedom and the freedom of hope. But this would be to invoke an inversion of the current state of affairs whereby the philosophical word of the white Australian would begin to be uttered against the background of the retreat of the historiographical word. Ultimately, from the standpoint of a future freedom, today's white Australia will be judged for the historian and the philosopher that it did not produce. Is there any more serious indictment than that of a failure of self-knowing? But this future has already arrived; it arrived with the occupation and its demands are already upon us. It is a matter of finding the courage to respond appropriately.

---

19. Lester-Irabinna Rigney, 'A First Perspective of Indigenous Australian Participation in Science: Framing Indigenous Research Towards Indigenous Australian Intellectual Sovereignty', *Kaurna Higher Education Journal*, vol.7, pp. 1-13 at p. 10.

3. THE 'HYPOTHETICAL NATION' AS BEING WITHOUT SOVEREIGNTY

The belief that white Australia would not have been an essentially different place were the land not already owned when the Europeans first arrived manifests a profound truth about white Australians. Without some continuing appeal to the idea of *terra nullius* white Australia could not continue to make sense of itself in ways that do not risk the shattering of its being. For, acting as its stable core, the idea of *terra nullius* supplies the white nation with its seeming integrity as a whole; through it white Australia perpetually exorcizes its being as that of the occupier. The historical violence we do to ourselves in denying who we really are ultimately grounds the depth of our commitment to the view that white Australia would have been essentially the same had the Indigenous peoples never existed.

But if this is correct, how might we explain the fact that white Australians have come to acknowledge the historical inaccuracy of the proposition that the land was indeed without sovereign owners when the Europeans first arrived?[20] The answer is that white Australians are great innovators where the doctrine of *terra nullius* is concerned. Commenting on its shifting meaning in white Australian law, Phillip Falk and Gary Martin cite the 1889 case of *Cooper v Stuart* to explain that judicial pronouncements had periodically endorsed an 'expanded doctrine'.

---

20. See for example, Henry Reynolds, *Aboriginal Sovereignty*, Australia, Penguin Books, 1996.

> This expanded doctrine reinterpreted *terra nullius* to mean 'without settled inhabitants or settled law', thus enabling the characterization of Aborigines as being nomads without civilized laws.[21]

But in more recent years the rejection of *terra nullius*—in both senses of an unoccupied land and of an unsettled land—has coincided with a more perverse extension of the meaning of this idea. It now serves to include Indigenous Australians as subjects *for whom* the land was originally unoccupied/unsettled. That is, far from abandoning reliance upon the idea of *terra nullius*, we have moved from an exclusionist understanding of *terra nullius*—one that presupposed the annihilation of the bearers of the question 'where do you come from?'—to a conception of *terra nullius for all*. This latter presupposes the annihilation of the question itself. Let us explain.

On our reading, the relevant historical turn took effect during the Whitlam years when in refining its relationship to difference and to otherness the white Australian state began to address two key social justice issues, one in relation to non-British migrants and the other in relation to Indigenous Australians. Whereas the first centered on the political state's relationship to ethnicity, the second confronted the question of land rights. Together, the two issues posed a challenge for the white Australian state to reorient its whiteness *as a whole*. That is, it had to engage in a process of redefinition and it did this by reformulating its self-understanding as a just social order, *this time* supposedly with the equal participation of all concerned. A new beginning was thus sought. Gough Whitlam's slogan 'It's Time' expressed exactly this.

In addressing the issue of ethnicity the political state affirmed the idea that it ought to stand in some neutral relationship to the ethnicities of its culturally diverse population. This was supposed to be a reasonable response to the demand that the state treat its citizens as equals under

---

21. Phillip Falk and Gary Martin, 'Misconstruing Indigenous Sovereignty: Maintaining the Fabric of Australian Law', in Aileen Moreton-Robinson (ed.), *Sovereign Subjects: Indigenous Sovereignty Matters*, NSW Australia, Allen and Unwin, 2007, pp. 33-46 at p. 37.

conditions of cultural pluralism. Of course, in practice a profound inequality continued to define state-citizen relations since the dominant British-Australian group had assigned itself the historical mission of managing the state's supposed neutrality. Nor did the Australian state's assertion of such a new beginning do away with the 'white straightjacket' that, as David Theo Goldberg shows in relation to 'racial states' in general, is the attire of an all-pervasive but invisible whiteness.[22] Although the Whitlam era introduced this new element in the self-awareness of the white Australian nation-state, it was the Fraser Government and the Labor governments of Hawke and Keating that developed it more fully. The era of Australian multiculturalism generated some anxiety for dominant white Australia precisely because, in adjusting to the idea (though not the reality) of state neutrality, the dominant group was no longer in a position to conflate the state's interests with those of one specific ethnicity, the British, as had been the practice since Federation. But Whitlam's 'It's Time' would inevitably lead us to John Howard's 'For All of Us'. Once the idea of the neutral state had been successfully tested in the public-political domain, the dominant Anglophone group progressively expanded its role from that of managing the state's neutrality to serving as the guarantor of the culturally diverse nation's unity. This was the logical conclusion of the process of development of a 'born-again' white Australia, to borrow another phrase from David Theo Goldberg.[23]

---

22. David Theo Goldberg, 'Racial states' in David Theo Goldberg (ed.), A Companion to Racial and Ethnic Studies, Massachusetts and Oxford, Blackwell, 233-258 at p. 235. See also David Theo Goldberg, *The Racial State*, Massachusetts and Oxford, Blackwell Publishers, 2002.

23. David Theo Goldberg, *The Threat of Race: Reflections on Racial Neoliberalism*, Malden MA, Oxford and Carlton Victoria, Wiley-Blackwell, 2009. For further discussion see Toula Nicolacopoulos and George Vassilacopoulos, 'Australian Multiculturalism: Beyond Management Models', in Reza Hasmath (ed.), *Managing Ethnic Diversity: Meanings and Practices from an International Perspective*, Surrey, Ashgate, 2011, pp. 141-176; Toula Nicolacopoulos and George Vassilacopoulos, 'Rethinking the Radical Potential of the Concept of Multiculturalism, in Tseen Khoo (ed.), *The Body Politic: Racialized Political Cultures in Australia (Refereed Proceedings*

The second issue, that of the ownership of the land, was also addressed on the presumption of a reformulated vision of equal citizenship that drew on a newly imagined original position in which all Australians are considered to be the co-creators of a just social order.[24] At the heart of this vision was the view that all Australians, and not just the whites, have an equal right to ownership of and belonging to this land. This new beginning was supposedly radical in so far as it sought to correct the historical injustice perpetrated against the Indigenous peoples. It helped to make the legal recognition of land rights, conceivable. Gary Foley explains,

> On 8 February [1972] the leader of the opposition, Gough Whitlam, [...] promised that a Labor Government would 'absolutely reverse' the government's policy on land rights, allowing 'ownership of land by tribal communities'. He also promised 'the introduction of a civil rights bill, overruling State laws that discriminated against Aborigines, a fully elected Legislative Assembly in the Northern Territory with a non-discrimination charter and free legal representation for Aborigines to test their rights in court. [...]
>
> Long before the Whitlam government met its downfall on 11 November 1975, Indigenous leaders had realized that there was a significant difference between the fine words and promises of Labor and the party's deeds.[25]

Indeed it was not possible to translate the words of Labor into white Australian deeds, despite Whitlam's implied affirmation of a new beginning. The reason is that the very idea of a new beginning itself presupposes that the continent is *terra nullius as a matter of principle for all concerned*, that is,

---

from the UQ Australian Studies Centre Conference, Brisbane, 24-26 November 2004), Brisbane and Melbourne, University of Queensland Australian Studies Centre, and Monash University National Centre for Australian Studies, 2005.

24. The philosopher John Rawls gave this idea a contemporary formulation in *A Theory of Justice* but its origins go back to seventeenth century Western formulations of citizen-state relations.

25. Gary Foley, 'The Australian Labor Party and the Native Title Act', citing Michael Mansell, pp. 123-125.

not just for the whites but for the blacks as well. Time frames and legalities aside, on this scenario both Indigenous and non-Indigenous Australians are equally imagined as 'settlers' on the continent. Chief Justice Brennan assumes as much when in the *Mabo* decision he analyzes the conditions under which 'our common law', the common law of a 'settled colony', would preclude recognition to its 'indigenous inhabitants' of their 'rights and interests in land'.[26] As the inhabitants of a settled colony governed by our common law, the Indigenous Australians are here *included* and can share in 'the benefits of settlement'. Such 'inclusion' of Indigenous Australians depends upon their accepting two underlying assumptions: the first is that colonial 'settlement' needn't have been secured *legally* and the second is that Indigenous claims to land *follow* colonial settlement, in a temporal sense. In other words, the Aborigines are rendered as latecomer settlers who can pursue land claims under our common law once the settler colony has illegally established itself. Ultimately, the ships that brought the Europeans here are now imagined to be big enough to accommodate not just those migrant groups who had previously been denied a place under the official *White Australia* policy, but also those whose histories place them here from time immemorial. This is the logical extension of a *terra nullius for all*. The activists who established the Aboriginal Tent Embassy did not need to await the *Mabo* decision to realize the perversity of the idea that sovereign peoples could be treated as settlers in their own homelands. In the words of Gary Foley,

> The period from 1967-1972 was a time when Indigenous activists were dramatically effective in their challenge to state and federal institutions, especially with the Aboriginal Tent Embassy protest on the lawns of Parliament House from January to July in 1972. The Tent Embassy was not simply a sit-in protest, but in fact was a demonstration of Aboriginal sovereignty. The underlying premise of the Tent Embassy was that Indigenous people regarded themselves as 'aliens in

---

26. *Mabo v the State of Queesnland*, (No.2) (1992) 175 CLR 1, at p. 31.

our own land', and therefore—like other sovereign nations—they would have an embassy to represent their interests in the federal capital.[27]

From the dual perspective of the operation of the ideas of a neutral state and a *terra nullius for all*, and in the name of a true equality, migrants claiming the right to preserve their specific cultures and Indigenous Australians who are represented as claiming limited land rights, come to be viewed on a par. By appealing to their original cultural specificities, both groups may call upon the supposedly neutral state to recognize and respect their differences and both may make demands upon the state in their capacity as co-creators of the nation and co-owner/occupiers of the land. It is this act of whitening the first Australians that misrepresents them in our present-future time frame as *one* group amongst the many who make up Australia.

In the words of Aileen Moreton-Robinson,

Indigenous people are never outside the discourse and power relations that produce us. We continuously experience such racialized moments in our daily encounters within a nation that is imagined as a white possession.[28]

As this 'white possession' the nation calls upon Aborigines to accept their own whitening, their place as co-creators of the new white Australian nation. As such co-creators we are now supposedly free to recognize our common origins in our desire to participate equally in this great social experiment. It follows from this imagined new beginning that Indigenous and white Australians must share a single answer to the question of our origins and this answer is given in terms of the ideals of justice and inclusiveness as these are ideally embodied in the white Australian nation-state. Far from presupposing any unconditional surrender to the rightful owners of the land, justice in such terms gives rise to calls for the insertion of Indigenous Australians into white Australia's already formulated understandings of a

---

27. Gary Foley, 'The Australian Labor Party and the Native Title Act', p. 123.

28. Aileen Moreton-Robinson, 'How White Possession Moves', pp. 230-231.

just social order as well as for their participation in the creation of a common history *from this point forward*.

Henceforth, it is *in the name of justice* that we attempt to annihilate the fundamental question at the core of the being of the occupier. Without exception, everyone is called upon today to construct his/her patriotic identity as a response to the supreme imperative of our shared whiteness, 'act as if the land were initially without owners'. For white Australia, this imperative is more primordial than the usual formulation of the call to patriotism, 'be prepared to sacrifice yourself for your country', since patriotic sacrifice presupposes that one already has a country to which one is devoted. The imperative of whiteness touches the depth of our ontology since it is from this that the white collective springs as the creator of the white Australian nation-state. White Australians perpetually enter the world in so far as we faithfully obey the imperative to act as if the land were initially without owners and it is through this imperative that we cover over the question 'where do you come from?' If this analysis is sound, then white Australia is unavoidably implicated in the perpetuation of the nation that must act 'as if ...' or what we call the 'hypothetical nation'. In Australia the idea of the hypothetical nation determines the imperative of whiteness.

The *as-ifology* we have described above haunts the white Australian collective precisely because the original owners are not only still here but they refuse to act hypothetically. Wendy Brady explains,

> When I think of myself, it is as a Wiradjuri. [...] The fantasised nation of Australia is just that a mythological place [...] it was claimed by the sovereign of a smaller island that bears no relationship to its name or naming to the Indigenous lands that are themselves sovereign nations. In contrast, Wiradjuri is country, family, history, heritage, spirituality, how to see the world, learn, understand belonging, be immersed in roles and responsibilities that define relationships to others of this Indigenous nation and guide body and soul.[29]

---

29. Wendy Brady, 'That Sovereign Being: History Matters', in Aileen Moreton-Robinson (ed.), *Sovereign Subjects: Indigenous Sovereignty Matters*,

In rejecting the hypothetical nation, Indigenous Australians appear as 'unpatriotic' and 'un-Australian', posing as internal threats to Australian national security.[30] But they also defiantly emerge before non-Indigenous Australians as the *only* genuine owners.

As a result of this encounter and in adhering to the imperative of whiteness, which has the power to shape the very character of our own being, the way we emerge in the world and as-a-world, our being has also been transformed into a *hypothetical being*. This is a being at whose core dwells an ontological emptiness, a great act of *kenosis* or emptying out of the very principle of self-determination that would otherwise define it. Indeed, it is this emptiness characterizing our hypothetically sovereign being that has dictated our collective destiny to date, a destiny that has given rise to a nation that is not merely conflicted but is incapable of actualizing its being as genuinely self-determining. Our claim then is that the empty being through which we have been gathering over the last two centuries is in fact a *being without sovereignty*.

What do we mean by 'sovereignty' in this context and why and in what sense does the white Australian nation-state presuppose the *kenosis* of this principle as a defining moment of its ontology? The starting point of a response to the first of these questions is the observation that our primary concern here is not with political/juridical sovereignty, in the sense of the formal-legal recognition between states or nations in the international political arena, but with *ontological* sovereignty. The way in which a collective primordially appears and announces itself as sovereign creator of a collective destiny implicates its members' emergence in the world and hence the question of sovereignty at the ontological level. As Wendy Brady explains, ontological sovereignty is both prior to juridical sovereignty and experienced as inalienable.

NSW Australia, Allen and Unwin, 2007, pp. 140-154 at p. 149.

30. See Toula Nicolacopoulos and George Vassilacopoulos, 'Rethinking the Radical Potential of the Concept of Multiculturalism', especially pp. 8-10.

We cannot relinquish our sovereign rights in relations to our lands, for it would mean denying our identity and connection to each other and the land that is the constitution of our being.

Every Indigenous Australian carries sovereignty within them. It is a product of being of the land and of the nation state. We are all sovereign Indigenous beings, and Western declarations of sovereignty are the myths of the colonisers to justify their occupation of Indigenous nation states.[31]

For white Australia then the prior question of ontological sovereignty arises as an outcome of the Indigenous-white Australian encounter. On the one hand, the very nature of the presence of the Indigenous peoples posits and sustains the principle of sovereignty. This follows from the fact of Indigenous resistance, the sovereign being's insistence upon posing the question 'where do you come from?' to the foreigner/invader, a fact that is born out by the colonizers' insistence on perpetuating the myth of *terra nullius* since there would have been no need knowingly to persist with the myth had the Indigenous peoples given up their sovereignty. On the other hand, Indigenous resistance provokes a violent return from the comfortable confines that the white Australian state has generated for its citizens to the originating entry point that determines the very institution of this state. In this way Indigenous resistance perpetually negates the white nation-state's claim of authority.

Like smoke from the rubble, the challenge that emerges before us is the very question of the being of a self-professed sovereign and self-instituting gathering. White Australians are first members of the white collective in this originating sense of a 'gathering-we', and only by extension citizens of the white Australian political state. If the Indigenous-white Australian encounter pushes white Australia in the direction of rethinking the fundamentals of the genealogy of our collective being, for historical reasons this translates into an appreciation of a certain modern Western European

---

31. Wendy Brady, 'That Sovereign Being: History Matters', p. 150.

ontological project, namely the project of a sovereign or self-determining gathering-we. Broadly speaking the gathering-we is the indeterminate but self-determining coming together of human beings who create and sustain economic, legal and above all political institutions and practices.[32] In order to identify the constitutive implications of this ontological project of sovereignty for the white Australian state, let us consider briefly the basic terms in which such a project has been activated historically.

---

32. For further discussion of the concept of the gathering-we see Toula Nicolacopoulos and George Vassilacopoulos, 'The Pulse of Chronos: Historical Time, the Eternal and Timelessness in the Platonic Gathering', *Parrhesia* vol.15, 2012, pp. 54-63.

4. A GENEALOGY OF THE WEST AS THE ONTOLOGICAL PROJECT OF THE GATHERING-WE

The emergence of the democratic city in ancient Greece makes possible a reading of the history of the West in terms of an epic story whereby Western Europeans engage ontologically with the gathering-we as a self-determining being. That is, we can make sense of the orientations and practices of such being in terms of a number of responses to certain commands to gather, commands that the gathering-we itself immanently activates from the times of the Greek *polis* onwards. For present purposes we can illustrate their workings by reference to four such commands: 'know thyself'; 'love each other'; 'be as a world'; and 'be as a person'. The first belongs to the ancient Greek gathering, the second to Christianity whereas the third is activate with the French Revolution. Each of these three commands addresses a community of sorts: the members of the *polis*, the community of believers, and the citizens as a universal collective. In contrast, the fourth command invokes the ethics and ontology of private property-owning individuals as distinct from the communities in which they function. Since Roman times, which explicitly codified private property-owning individuality by turning it into a legal mode of being, the command to 'be as a person' progressively functions as the dominant field in relation to which the other three commands present as unsuccessful alternatives and challengers.

The Athenian gathering of Socrates and the friends of the philosopher was the first explicit manifestation of the sovereign being of the gathering-we understood as a response to the command to 'know thyself'. As a democracy that accommodated (some) free individuals, the Greek *polis* was perhaps in a unique position to enact a philosophical form of the gathering *as such* as happened when Socrates introduced the *polis* to a philosophical formulation of the idea of gathering *as a project to be realized*. By positing himself as the bearer of the very idea of the gathering and as the *topos* of gathering for the friends of the philosopher, Socrates posed a fundamental challenge to the gathering of the Athenian citizens, a challenge for which he was ultimately prepared to sacrifice his own life. Here the vision was for the gathering to institute itself out of a state of indeterminate sovereign being, that is, to create appropriate institutions, or to form a determinate gathering, by unconditionally receiving the command to 'know thyself'. In constituting the being of the gathering—its emerging as gathering—such a response was to function as the presupposition for (re)instituting the *polis*.

The Athenian *polis* took up the philosopher's challenge in a way that inaugurates the ontological history of the West. Henceforth, the West confronts its being by repeatedly undermining its very principle of self-determination. In the case of Athens, this was done through the annihilation of the bearer of the principle, namely the indeterminate gathering of the philosopher and his friends. In condemning the philosopher to death, the gathering-we constituted as the Greek *polis* henceforth gathers through a denial of the very idea of gathering. So, from the outset of its emergence as sovereign and self-determining, the gathering of the West announces itself as the power of explicit self-denial and as the practice of this denial. Western being thus constitutes itself as this sort of double act of an infinitely violent *kenosis* (emptying of being).

It is in this ontological tension that a second great project of the West is activated, namely that of visionary philosophy.

Philosophy emerges as the vision of the sovereign gathering-we and as this vision it exposes the practice of self-denial amongst the members of the gathering of the *polis*. The first master of this intellectual project is Plato and his masterpiece is *The Republic*. *The Republic* is the manifesto of one who rebels against the practice of *kenosis*, and a meditation on the very idea of gathering understood in the above terms. On this reading of Plato the indeterminate gathering and its corresponding vision manifest in the embrace of the philosopher whose connection with the *Agathon* (supreme good) enables him at once to create the *polis* anew and to function as its ruler. In Plato's ideal *polis* the ontological tension is overcome once everyone responds to the command to 'know thyself' by dwelling in the philosopher's embrace. The gathering in question is a sovereign one in so far as it incorporates in its being its knowing and hence the principle of its self-institution. Such a response makes possible, firstly, the formation of the sovereign indeterminate *gathering-we of the philosopher and his friends* that is at once the bearer and the response to the command; and, secondly, the institutions of the just *polis* that flow from this self-determining gathering. Here for the first time in the West the individual is conceived, firstly, as a member of the indeterminate gathering that institutes its sovereign being through the sovereign act of responding to the command to 'know thyself'; and, secondly, as a citizen of the enacted *polis*.[33]

Following the Greeks, a second historical emergence of the indeterminate gathering-we responds to the Christian command to 'love each other'. Here a decisive difference marks the gathering of the community of love from that of Plato's just *polis*. Although each appeals to a supreme source of significance—the *Agathon* and the Christian God respectively—for the community of love it is not just one person, the philosopher, but every believer who is positioned to be in touch with this source. Consequently, every member of the

---

33. For further elaboration see George Vassilacopoulos, 'Plato's *Republic* and the End of Philosophy', *Philosophical Inquiry*, vol. XIX, no.1-2, 2007, pp. 34-45.

gathering-we of believers functions as the *topos* of the indeterminate gathering of love, that is as a gatherer and not just as gathered together. Even so, the instituted forms of gathering amongst the Christians no less manifest the West's self-denial. In so far as they practice a denial of the self-determining power of the indeterminate gathering-we of the believers, the order(s) of Christians are ultimately reduced to the servants of the state, or themselves act as the secular and oppressive state.

The universal equality and bond to which the Christian project gives rise is subsequently radicalized with the French Revolution. This in turn marks a third version of the Western ontological project, this time in European modernity. The Revolution invokes the command to 'be as free and equal in accordance with solidarity', or what we can reformulate more generally as 'be as-a-world'. In the formation of the being of *the gathering-we as solidarity* each member of the collective potentially functions as the place of dwelling for the other members. This new ontological opening radically democratizes the mediating role that in Socrates' practice and in Plato's ideal *polis* was confined to the philosopher. In responding to the command to 'be as-a-world' the collective emerges through a practice in which the members mutually recognize one another in a dual capacity: each dwells *in* the other and also serves as the place of dwelling *for* the other. Here the individuality of the subject is constituted in the dynamic interaction of infinite expansion, in embracing the others, and of infinite contraction, in being embraced by the other. This dynamic interaction grounds the emergence of the collective in solidarity via a practice of mutual recognition.

By contrast, the *gathering-we of private property owners*, the gathering that responds to the command to 'be as a person', substitutes the dual embracing that defines the ontology of solidarity with that of the emerging and merging of otherwise exclusive individual subjects. In this case I emerge in the world by owning something specific, by claiming it as exclusively mine and, in doing so, claiming my emerging and unique being as exclusively mine. At the same time as emerging in this pure self-recognition and self-ownership that manifests as the power of saying 'I' and 'mine', the individual also merges with others in the equality of sameness that comes with recognizing the private property-owning capacity of every other subject like me. Through this particular practice of the mutual recognition of the absolute self-ownership of each individual, private property owners institute their indeterminate gathering-we by reading the command to be as-a-world in the specific terms: 'be as the world of private property owners'. It is the response to this formulation of the command that has given rise to the myth of the social contract—a story of the gathering-we as consisting of self-interested individuals who form and endorse their institutions as a result of rational agreement—which nonetheless presupposes its source in the *indeterminate* gathering-we, albeit without appreciating this.

One noteworthy difference between the two abovementioned responses to the command to be as-a-world in Western modernity by comparison with the gathering-we of the believers and that of the Greek *polis* is that the former do not appeal to a supreme good that is located beyond the gathering itself. It is at this point that a decisive radicalization takes place in connection with the idea of *ontological sovereignty*. Henceforth, to be sovereign is to ground the subject's (individual or collective) being, or emerging, in the act of emerging itself. Just as when in love one appears as a loving being in the very act of loving, so too one emerges in the world as a sovereign being in the very practice of sovereignty and not as an effect of one's relationship to some *externally derived* values, institutions or authorities.

This said the dual processes of instituting the gathering-we of solidarity and of private property owners manifest their own forms of self-denial. Historically, whereas the social revolutionary movements have resulted in undermining the very principle of solidarity they have sought to implement, the liberal-capitalist democracies that have sprung out of the indeterminate gathering of private property owners have taken shape through the dispossession, colonization and enslavement of others, even as their fundamental principles implicitly acknowledge the sovereign gathering-we as the originating source of *every* socially instituted gathering-we. In denying to other beings and social orders what they presuppose to be universal—the sovereign being of private property ownership *as such*—modern Western liberal-capitalist orders also undermine their own sovereign and self-determining being and implicate this being in the *kenosis* of its defining principle of sovereignty.

Given its importance to our present discussion we will explain three key features of the ontology of private property ownership, namely the relationship of owning to nature, to the future, and to the modern Western nation-state. Let us begin by noting that in owning a thing it is not the specificity of the thing owned, for example, this piece of land, this tree, and so on, that is revealed through such owning. Even though what I own is indeed a specific thing, its ownability has less to do with its specificity and more to do with its mode of being, namely its indifference. That is, within the ontology of modern Western private property ownership, that the thing is owned entails that it is indifferent to itself. The attribution of indifference to the thing takes place through the thing's positioning in the wider scheme of things or what is referred to as *nature*. For the subject who implicitly or explicitly defines agency through private ownership, *nature as such* is essentially defined by the mode of being of indifference, both to itself and to the subject.

From this perspective ownership acquires cosmic proportions. That I own this thing means that as owner I open up nature's mode of being allowing everything natural to be situated within this horizon and hence to be shaped by the absolute indifference of nature. Hence, even before it is directed towards specific need satisfaction through purposive use, in its capacity as private possession, owning constitutes the ontological practice of making explicit nature's indifference. Now because from this perspective qua mode of being nature's indifference is universal, the practice of owning along with the associated agency involved in such practice and the response to the command to 'be as a person' are all seen as genuinely universal projects. Under appropriate conditions, this orientation in turn gives rise to the colonizing drive given that the ultimate aim here is to (re)construct the totality of the world in conformity with the (onto)logic of nature's indifference.

For reasons that we need not examine here, the logic belonging to the agent who opens up the universal field of nature's indifference through the practice of owning, consists of the formalism characterizing mathematical thinking. Mathematical thinking is the precondition of and gives rise to another implication of the owner's relation to nature, namely the modern Western techno-scientific project. If it is possible to open up nature's mode of being then all the specifics of nature are in principle knowable and potentially re-creatable. It follows from this that in the mathematical knowing and re-creating of nature (science and technology), the techno-scientific project perpetually reveals the indifference of nature that is enacted through owning. Of course this means that nature is here experienced as a 'something' that is empty of any immanent significance and hence as potentially open to being endlessly manipulated.

It is interesting to note that the techno-scientific enactment of nature's indifference, although sharing lines of continuity, also involves an important shift whereby the modern Western project of the universal gathering of owners distances itself from the specific orientation to nature that manifests in the particularistic *polis* of ancient Greece. Here we can draw upon Plato, and in particular his story of the cave in *The Republic*, to give a sense of the difference in the way in which the Greeks took the mode of being of nature to be its indifference.[34] When Plato's philosopher leaves the

---

34. In Plato's story of the Cave society consists of a group of cave dwellers whose movements, and hence access to knowledge, are severely restricted until one of them, the philosopher, having broken free of his chains, makes his way out into the light of the Sun and acquires true knowledge of the absolute good. He then returns to the Cave to share the benefits of his experience with his fellow cave dwellers. See Toula Nicolacopoulos and

cave and his fellow cave dwellers to move out into the light of the Sun, he comes to experience the perfect indifference of the *Agathon*. Unlike the modern techno-scientific relationship to the natural world, the indifferent here is not discovered as something to be manipulated. Rather the perfectly indifferent is appreciated as the source of life. Here we have, not the revealing of the indifference of nature through the practice of owning, but reverence toward the indifferent through the practice of observing its function as an all-inclusive horizon. The important point for us is that Plato thought that if the members of the human gathering, the philosopher's fellow cave dwellers, failed to appreciate the observable, indifferent *Agathon*, an appreciation that had to be facilitated by their link to the wisdom brought to them by the philosopher upon returning to the cave, they would regrettably immerse themselves in the practice of unlimited owning thereby unleashing an inevitable drive towards imperialism. For, the subject who practices unlimited owning activates a mode of being defined in terms of the problem of having to satisfy infinite needs through finite means of satisfaction. For Plato, this constitutes a practice of ignorance and, hence, of self-denial given that it is the human gathering expressing itself as a particular and hence limited form of togetherness—the mode of being of the *polis*—that is in a position to appreciate the *Agathon*. The gathering that does not have access to this wisdom, not only fails to appreciate its own limits and boundaries, it also seeks to expand by penetrating the boundaries of others. This drive ultimately destroys, not only other gatherings but also its very own. The destruction in question is of course both physical and spiritual. Plato's solution was to seek to design the just *polis* so as to ensure that it remains powerful and wise enough to contain and harness the imperialistic and self-destructive tendencies of the ontology of private property-owning that was emerging within the context of the particularistic community. He may well have been the first to sense and react against the latent imperialist drive that is immanent in the orientation of the West. Perhaps he was also the first to sense that the 'novelty' of the West was one of *thanatology*, that is, of self-destruction and self-denial ontologically produced through the enactment of private ownership.

This brings us to the second feature of the modern universalizing practice of owning, namely its relationship to the future. The legalized practice of private property-owning, which became universal *in-principle* under the Romans, leaves behind the Platonic gathering's orientation towards the particularistic community, the limited solidarity found in the life of the *polis*. With the legal expression of private property, the Romans elevate the practice of owning to a fundamental norm of recognition between humans and between humans and nature. The completion of this project around the fifteenth century also makes it possible to activate the techno-scientific drive to conquer nature (and society). Over time, these two projects were progressively supplemented by the development of corresponding economic and political institutions that embody the abstract universality of the private property owner, the alignment of the universal human subject with the identity of the private property owner in the radical sense of having been rendered as an essentially empty vessel, the pure 'I' that is detached from all substantive meaning-generating ties. We can now identify a paradox at the heart of the current global project of private property-owning, whose source traces back to the Romans and which develops through various complex waves that we need not examine here. With these developments, the world of the private property owner is posited as the world of the *perpetual present*, a present that has both displaced the past, whether in terms of the solidarity of the *polis* or the loving community of the believers, and made redundant, once and for all, the utopian future of solidarity—the all-encompassing solidarity of the indeterminate gathering of the future—that the French revolutionaries announced. Here we encounter the liberal-capitalist and techno-scientific triumph of the private person who thinks of himself or herself as living the end of history.

But the abovementioned negation of the future, the rejection of the command to 'be as a world', is at once the emptying out from within its own being of the subject's erotic moment of fusion with the universal gathering of solidarity. As a result of this *kenotic* act the private property owner confronts the gathering through the rejection of any possibility of expanding and thereby embracing the collective. The 'miracle' of the unique individual, who, in the capacity of a responsible participant of the gathering, expands infinitely to embrace the gathering and nature, is alien to the ontology of the private property owner. This being is thus posited as monadic and private, holding the secret of its supreme insignificance.

Through the rejection of the substantive universality characterizing the future understood in terms of a global solidarity and the substitution in its place of the empty universality of the measurable and the endlessly measured, private property-owning subjectivity effectively retreats into a new mode of particularity. This is evidenced with the emergence of universalist liberal states within the horizon of particularistic nations. The third feature of the modern universalizing practice of owning, the modern Western nation, gives concrete substance to the otherwise empty being of the universalist state formations. As we noted above, the enactment of private property-owning subjectivity, which is governed by the endless multiplication of needs and desires whose satisfaction is limited by the availability of finite resources, accords with expansionism, colonization and the dispossession of other peoples pursuant to the drive to turn the whole earth into a field for the exploitation of resources. At the same time, through its nationalistic particularity property-owning subjectivity comes out of its private sphere of insignificance, attaches arbitrarily to some territory and imposes boundaries as the rightful domain of the nation. This supreme expression of national ownership, which derives from the tension between the abovementioned universalistic and particularistic drives, gives a determinate shape to the imperialistic / colonizing tendencies of the techno-scientific liberal-capitalist projects.

Ultimately, before reducing the other to a 'thing' and thereby denying the other the fundamental private property-owning power, colonial subjectivity has already denied to itself the all-encompassing solidarity of the indeterminate gathering. As un-loved and non-loving the colonial subject hides the depth of his or her ontological emptiness by engaging in criminal activity the world over. Having reduced the core of one's own being to a vessel of infinite self-directed violence with the denial of a global future of solidarity, the colonial subject then enacts violence against all others whose acts of solidarity serve as the perpetual ground for the repetition of this self/other directed violence. Even though the mark of the truly sovereign private property owner is, neither the satisfaction of insatiable desires nor the freedoms secured by the techno-scientific project, but the willingness to sacrifice oneself in order to protect the ontological integrity of the being of the owner, a being that cannot be reduced to slavery, nevertheless in enslaving others the property owner also secures one's own enslavement. Far from affirming one's ontological sovereignty then the property owner abandons this very sovereignty in the name of practicing it. This violent nihilism transforms itself into the nihilism of violence.

5. ONTOLOGICAL SOVEREIGNTY AND THE HOPE OF A WHITE AUSTRALIAN PHILOSOPHY OF ORIGINS

In so far as white Australia embodies the project of the West in the broad terms we have sketched, the ontology of the gathering-we of private property owners decisively shapes its destiny. Within such a framework the individual cannot merely embrace items of property for their discrete mediating power, the power that enables one to claim one's individual being as their own. Rather, the individual must also embrace the command to 'be as-a-world of property owners' as this manifests in the practice of instituting the legal, economic, and political arrangements in accordance with the mutual recognition of property owners. Yet, if our analysis is sound, to date the destiny of white Australians has been shaped not by the will to respond to this command with integrity but by conformity to the imperative of whiteness. That is, rather than engaging directly with the command to be as-a-world of property owners, white Australia responds through the 'as if' imperative. Not 'be as-a-world' but 'in order to be as-a-world act as if the land were initially without owners'. Consequently, far from being self-instituting, the being of the gathering of white Australians is decisively *without sovereignty*; its freedom has been compromised. Ironically, our being is thus flooded with property just as it empties itself of the power of self-ownership. It is the being of a collective subject that claims to own property yet is incapable of owning its being as manifested in this property simply because that which is claimed as one's own already belongs to another. The emptiness that derives from conformity to the imperative of whiteness thus consists in the absence of ontological sovereignty and in the absoluteness of this absence.

This explains why, in giving rise to the demand that white Australia give a truthful account of its origins, the Indigenous-white Australian encounter also calls upon white Australians to confront the question of ownership first and foremost as an ontological issue in the above sense. Such a demand radically transforms the white Australian on one level at the same time as leaving us intact on another. For, it does not deny our private property-owning identity *as such*; it rather denies to white Australia the rightful ownership of something very specific, Australian territory. So, in forcing white Australia to relate explicitly to the very idea or principle that shapes the being of the gathering-we of property owners, the encounter affirms our private property-owning capacity whilst simultaneously exposing the self-denial inherent in the enactment of our private property-owning identity. This is the ontological fate of white Australians as property owners to the extent that private property ownership remains the dominant mode of being at the global scale.

In so far as we fail to address the ontological and world-making significance of private property ownership we also fail to live up to the self-professed ideals of Western liberal modernity. This is another formulation of our paradoxical or contradictory state, the state of the 'as if'. White Australia proudly claims to be a fully modern Western nation yet is incapable of being one in practice. For, we violate the fundamentals of our ontology at the same time as invoking them to make sense of ourselves individually and collectively. We perpetually suffer from an ontological pathology, what we call 'onto-pathology', by simultaneously embracing and abandoning the Western ontological project of sovereign being. White Australia has been shaped by this great failure. This is the paradox that we must confront, not by reflecting on historical data, but by becoming immersed in the drama of our ontology. At the center of this ontological drama, the white nation unfolds as the outcome of a *kenosis* of sovereignty and this great lack of sovereignty manifests as a gathering of the property owners responsible for instituting the white Australian state through the practices that have enabled us to call this land, the only land most of us will ever know, 'our country'.

Is there a way out? How might we white Australians begin to distance ourselves from the imperative of our whiteness? What would be the effect of listening to the transcending power of the words 'where do you come from?' and making the ontological leap of naming our being as empty of sovereignty? The naming of our being as empty would be a supreme moment of wisdom, the only available response to the question 'where do you come from?' Let us proceed then to explore the possibility of such naming in the form of a philosophical exercise.

6. THE WORLD-MAKING SIGNIFICANCE OF PROPERTY OWNERSHIP IN WESTERN MODERNITY

We have been arguing that we open ourselves to the world of modern Western instituted society as free and sovereign subjects—operating in market relations, as legal subjects and as citizens of a liberal political state—in so far as we act as private property owners. The notion of private property ownership plays such a crucial role at the ontological level of white Australian encounters in and as-a-world because the idea of the subject as a property-owning identity defines the fundamental relationship between the subject of Western modernity and his or her world. In what follows we will explore the ontological orientation that private property-owning subjects must take in so far as we seek to emerge as a response to the question 'where do you come from?'. We will proceed by drawing upon a Hegelian conception of modern property-owning subjectivity, which, for reasons that we need not go into here, informs the very structure or *form* of subjectivity that underpins the discourses of property ownership governing contemporary life.[35]

When we think of the individual subject just in relation to its form, we focus on the pure capacity to be a subject who claims ownership over his or her own doing and being or, what we earlier referred to as the self-ownership that underpins the modern Western subject's capacity for saying

---
35. G.W.F. Hegel, *Philosophy of Right*, trans. T.M. Knox, Oxford, Oxford University Press, 1967, § 34-104.

'I' and 'mine'. Let us refer to this capacity of the subject as 'the subject's formal or abstract being'. In its most basic form this subject is sovereign and self-determining but this self-determining power of subjectivity is wholly abstract. It is grounded in an immediate self-centered awareness, as expressed in the personal pronoun 'I' without further qualification. This immediate awareness of self supplies us with *the form* of our being-as-a-world; it constitutes us as *formally free* and this is the framework of possibilities within which we actively position ourselves to all the specificities of our embodiment including race, ethnicity, gender, class, sexuality and so on. The modern Western subject's formal freedom is empty in the sense of being conceived as lacking any *pre-given* substantive specific determinations of this kind. This does not necessarily mean that the subject is somehow imagined to have a disembodied existence apart from their personal socially constructed history—a history that is inevitably implicated in specific (colonial, class, sexual, race, gender) relations—but rather that the being of the subject, that does indeed exist with all the particular determinations that make up its unique history, is nevertheless not reducible to (the sum of) these particulars. There is more to the subject than these distinct details and this more is conceived as the singular site of the power of self-determination. Indeed, one implication of the emptiness of formal subjectivity as we are describing it here is that it empowers the subject to generate its own needs and desires, rather than merely to pursue their satisfaction as the givens of its existence, of its place or time. Moreover, precisely because it is *I* who makes any particular need or desire mine, I can keep generating new needs and desires for myself just as I can disavow others.

Conceiving a subject in this way, also gives rise to a corresponding relationship to the world. Here, the world takes the form simply of whatever is *external to* the subject or, in other words, the world is the 'externality' of the subject's abstract being. For the private property-owning subject then everything that is placed beyond one's own abstract being—whatever falls into the category of the *non-I*—has the potential to be transformed into something that belongs to the subject's external world. So, for example, amongst the myriad ways in which I might speak of the human body in my own case, one of these ways presupposes that (parts of) it fall(s) outside the scope of what I invoke when I say 'I', at least in principle, and this holds for anything specific that I can identify about me and my world.

Focusing on the emptiness of the subject's formal freedom allows us to appreciate another important implication for the private property-owning subject's way of being in the world. Significantly, this subject-world relationship makes the being of all particulars a matter of their *accessibility* to the subject. That is, for the private property-owning subject whatever happens to fall outside the site of its abstract being is worthy of existence to the extent that it is (potentially) *visible* to the subject. So, the modern Western subject's abstract self-relation manifests the subject's very power to re-conceive and organize the world in a way that enables the subject to affirm itself in it. In other words, the world is already implicated in the subject's power of abstraction as the world *of the subject*; as the world that exists to serve the subject. The subject's activity of abstracting—the movement from its specificities to its abstract being—is, therefore, the point of potentiality out of which to create reality in conformity with the subject's self-centered awareness.

In this way, the subject's power of self-determination is formulated in terms of something to be achieved, as a project, rather than as a given. Unlike the epistemological awareness of the Cartesian subject that progressively leaves behind every specific aspect of the world in a (futile) effort to achieve self-certainty, the Hegelian subject's awareness is not trapped in its own internal space; it does not imply a problematically disembodied relationship to the world. Rather, the driving force through which it is constituted from the outset is best formulated as what we might call 'the will-to-be'. This is why, for Hegel, the first imperative of the subject is: '*be* as a person'.[36]

---

36. G.W.F. Hegel, *Philosophy of Right*, § 36, emphasis added.

By implicating the world in its abstracting activity the modern Western subject makes manifest the fundamental terms of its potential being in the world. From its position of a will-to-be, understood in the above terms, the external world—everything beyond the self-centered awareness of the subject—is constituted as its *immediate other* in a dual sense. The external world is both *irreducibly different* and the *separable* other of the subject. So, from the standpoint of the will-to-be, the immediate other of the subject must be constituted as that which exists *without a will of its own*. This is what Hegel refers to as 'the thing'. The Hegelian thing is a specificity, any particular whatsoever, that the subject positions as indifferent to itself in the sense of incapable of taking an active interest in itself. This indifference to itself renders the external thing as capable of *receiving a will* from the outside, so to speak. In so far as the thing is in itself empty of will it can be conceived as something at once penetrable and separable. This enables the subject positioned as the will-to-be to exercise choice about inhabiting the thing under appropriate conditions.

Within this conceptual framework, the thing is just as much an abstraction as the category of the formally free subject out of which it is derived. Their difference lies in the idea that the latter actively draws upon the former; the will that is empty of embodied being depends for its own self-determined emerging upon the thing that exists as empty of will. This relation of dependence is at the heart of the ontology of the property relation. It enables us to embody our own will in the thing and thereby to transform the thing into our own (exclusive) property. As external to the being of the abstract subject, every thing in the external world is potentially an item of private property just as every embodied subject is potentially a private property owner. This is what enables the modern Western subject to treat all manner of relations, not merely as *analogous* to property understood in some more restricted sense, but as *essentially* private property relations. In this structure of relations, anything that is positioned as non-I is potentially transformable into private property. Indeed, my nation, my children, my ethnicity, my body(parts), my skills, talents, ideas, are all capable of being transformed into private property, to the extent that I position them as external to my formal being. As Cheryl Harris explains, whiteness itself has been transformed into property.[37]

To be sure, there are many reasons for opposing this formulation of the subject-world relation. But, to the extent that it underpins the institutions of Western modernity, we are implicated in its logic irrespective of whether we disapprove of this logic at an intellectual level. That is, even if we disagree with its implications, for example, in allowing us to treat the natural and social worlds as lacking a spirit of their own, this construction of the world, and the world's consequent de-spiritualization, are currently indispensable to the ways in which modern Western subjects encounter the world. As the will-to-be in the world, formally free subjects unavoidably de-spiritualize a world they presuppose as the world of particular things. For, willful exclusive possession of what was previously a will-less thing constitutes the primary form of embodiment for modern Western subjectivity; it is invoked whenever we assert: 'this is mine'.

---

37. Cheryl I. Harris, 'Whiteness as Property', *Harvard Law Review*, vol. 106, no. 8, 1993, pp. 1707-1791; *UCLA School of Law Research Paper*, no. 06-35, available at SSRN: http://ssrn.com/abstract=927850 .

7. SOVEREIGN BEING AND THE ENACTMENT OF PROPERTY OWNERSHIP

Significantly for our discussion, the form of embodiment we have been describing takes place *immediately* in the sense of not relying on any mediation by another; the embodiment in question must establish a direct relation between the subject and the possession of some thing. The immediacy inherent in the act of taking possession of a thing gives concrete being to formal subjectivity in a crucial way. It constitutes the subject as a *self-grounded* presence. That is, in becoming what I am through my own act of will, and without the direct involvement of another will, I achieve for myself a kind of grounding that enables me to relate securely to myself as an embodied being and to my particular place in the world. This kind of self-grounding underpins modern Western ideals of cosmopolitan life styles which enable people to move freely and selectively between and across multiple and diverse sites of socio-cultural engagement. But it is also at the heart of the modern Western feeling of belonging to a certain place and of identifying with a site as one's own 'home'. The significance of achieving one's self-grounded being is further highlighted when it is violated, for example, through arbitrary restrictions to one's free movements or invasions to privacy.

This said, the subject-world relation we have been describing also harbors a certain contradiction since at the same time as calling for immediate (unmediated) possession, in the above mentioned way, every individual act of embodiment of a will in a thing is after all mediated in that it inevitably implicates another will. In transforming the thing into my exclusive property through its immediate possession I extend myself into it and render it the site of my embodied being, but within the framework of the logic of private property, this property must still remain alienable. That is, it must always be capable of being transferred to another private property-owning subject. The maintenance of this sort of distance between the subject and its particular property items is necessary for preserving the formal freedom inherent in this way of being. Without the alienability of property the exercise of this formal being leaves open the possibility of being locked into the concrete particularity of the specific thing. This is why the practice of claiming something to be mine, or embodiment of my will in the thing, also depends upon there being another private property-owning subject to whom my property is potentially transferable. The relationship therefore presupposes the *mutual recognition* of private property-owning subjects with the potential to exchange their property.

Hence, the logic that defines the relationship of the private property-owning subject to its external world does not only construct this world in terms of particular will-less things but also renders the mutual recognition of private property-owning subjects as an indispensable feature of the kinds of social interaction that this world hosts. Indeed, as modern Western subjects, we encounter others *as subjects* by recognizing them as private property-owning identities. Because exchange relations manifest this fundamental form of mutual recognition, their on-going re-enactment plays the role of affirming our way of being in Western modernity just as custom and religion might do in different socio-historical contexts. In our secularized world that has broken its essential ties with tradition, the recognition of formal subject-to-subject relations ultimately invokes the idea of the will-less thing instead.

In so far as we are implicated in this open field shaped by the mutual informing of the practices of immediate possession and mediated recognition, we effectively dwell in the space of emerging of the indeterminate gathering of private property-owning subjects. Hence, what is absolutely singular and unique, the being of each private property-owning 'I', is also engaged in instituting a certain collective being that makes possible and necessary the uttering of the 'we' by the 'I'. The very logic of the emerging of one's sovereign being renders each specific person as a property owner *in general*. This is what makes exchange possible. Here exchange is grounded not just on the exchangeability of the thing that can be given a (monetary) value but also on the fact that the participants are the bearers of the very idea of formal, private property-owning subjectivity and consequently are in a position to merge with each other in the appropriate sense of a shared property-owning being; they are thus positioned to utter the 'we' in terms of the exchange relations to which their property-owning being gives rise. In so far as the indeterminate gathering-we of property owners transforms itself into an *instituted gathering-we*, as defined by the practice of mutual recognition amongst its bearers, the being of such a gathering emerges as sovereign and self-determining.

This is how the command to 'be as a person' is radicalized in taking the form: 'be as-a-world of persons'. To respond to this command then is to respond to the call for certain world-creating possibilities. It is to emerge as the bearer of the absolute right of my own self-determining being in a world constituted in common with the other bearers of this right. Significantly, this ontological right functions not only as the ground and point of reference for all the other rights that become part of the fabric of the self-instituting gathering-we of property owners, but also as the ground of sacrifice for the protection of the being of personality itself. The right of private property-owning persons has sometimes been represented as inalienable, as inherent to being human, leading to confusion about the relationship between personality and property with the protection of, or threat to, life. For John Locke, for example, the authority of a liberal social order rests with its power to protect the inalienable right of individuals to life, liberty and property.[38] But, from the standpoint of the absolute right of the self-instituting gathering-we of property owners that we have been elaborating, it is not the protection of life but the possibility of sacrificing one's life that is at the heart of being as-a-world of persons.

From this perspective, the primary concern is not to recognize that property ownership flows from mixing one's labor with the earth, as is sometimes argued following Locke, but to recognize instead the significance of someone's willingness to mix the earth with their blood in order to defend their own and others ontological right to be. Such a right affirms its absolute authority, and the freedom and sovereignty associated with this, only if the life of the emerging being of the property owner springs from the liberating possibility of sacrifice for the sake of this very right. In other words, the absolute authority of the right to be is grounded in the fact that it claims our being *as a whole* absolutely. In the absence of the readiness to sacrifice oneself to protect one's ontological integrity such a fundamental right would remain empty. Hence the command 'be as-a-world' is itself premised on a prior and more fundamental command: 'in order to be worthy of being as-a-world of persons be prepared to sacrifice yourself for your right to be a person'. The willingness to sacrifice one's life is therefore a defining act of the individual's sovereign being, and for that matter of the sovereignty of the gathering-we.

---

38. John Locke, *Two Treatises of Government*, (1689), P. Laslett (ed.), Cambridge, Cambridge University Press, 1988.

8. THE ONTO-PATHOLOGY OF WHITE AUSTRALIAN SUBJECTIVITY

We have been arguing, not just that from the standpoint of Western modernity, property and sovereignty are inseparable issues, but that from the outset they have flooded the ontological space created by the Indigenous-white Australian encounter. Indeed, when we take seriously the modern Western ontological orientation to these issues, we may well wonder whose stand really accords with the being that has been constituted as inescapably property-owning, those who have mixed their labor with the earth or those who have shed their blood on and for this land? Who, after all, are the bearers of sovereign being, those who defend their emerging in the world, and hence the sovereignty of their self-instituting being, or those who practice a retreat from this emerging? We want to go on next to explain the process by which, despite being unavoidably constituted as property-owning subjects under the conditions of Western modernity, white Australians have indeed retreated from their *sovereign* emerging as property-owning beings. This retreat, we will suggest, takes place through a practice of simultaneously perpetrating *ontological violence* against the Indigenous other as well as *ontological terror* against ourselves. In explaining these phenomena and considering their implications for the constitution of our being as *white Australian* we do not focus on identifying and ordering the relevant historical facts but on unpacking the meaning-generating implications of the phenomena in question. To this end, our discussion offers a way of understanding our connections with the violence, racism and resistance that define the Indigenous-white Australian encounter.

Let us begin by considering in what way the violence perpetrated against the Indigenous peoples constitutes more than an admittedly serious injustice on a moral or ethical plane. In the present context the distinct significance of what we are referring to as 'ontological violence' concerns the fundamental question of mutual recognition in the terms already discussed. With the violent dispossession of the Indigenous peoples white Australia did more than merely fail to acknowledge the status of Indigenous Australians as the country's original owners, as has been suggested.[39] For the Indigenous-white Australian encounter is not just a matter of the latter denying to the former their rights of control over their lands. Instead, white Australia has denied Indigenous being as self-determining subjects and as sovereign peoples. This is not to suggest that the Indigenous peoples depend upon the white Australian state for recognition of their sovereign being. As Tony Birch explains,

> sovereignty within Indigenous communities themselves is not reliant on either European law or occasional state paternalism. It is maintained through pre-existing, pre-European models of governance.[40]

Nevertheless, this self-sustaining internal sovereignty has been rendered inoperative in Indigenous - white Australian relations and the refusal fully to recognize Indigenous property-owning being is a constitutive feature of the relationship.

To be sure, historically the refusal to recognize the Indigenous property-owning being has been justified on ideological grounds that drew upon racist notions of British supremacy to formulate and willfully perpetuate the myth of *terra nullius* in its various manifestations. But, let us put aside the question of the accuracy of this account of the

---

39. See, for example, Genevieve Lloyd, 'No one's Land'.
40. Tony Birch, 'The Invisible Fire', p. 107.

reasoning that must have informed the colonizers' actions at a certain point in time. When we focus instead on the private property-owning structure of subjectivity that is presupposed for the deployment of this myth, we can begin to appreciate the deeper meaning or significance of the myth's *willful perpetuation*. From this perspective it becomes clear that we cannot make full sense of the being of the occupier by insisting that the colonizers were interested in grounding colonial self-presence in a territory that *presented* as will-less, as a land without owners, because it was mistakenly viewed as unoccupied or as unsettled. Such an act would indeed have constituted an attempt to affirm the colonizers' own private property-owning being without posing any risk to their ontological integrity, since taking possession of an otherwise will-less thing manifests the seminal desire for unmediated embodiment. But this scenario ignores the fact of Indigenous resistance, a fact that betrays a deep ontological tension given that Indigenous resistance alerted the colonizers to their misrecognition. Indeed, the desire for unmediated possession did manifest in the actions of those colonists who, contrary to the myth's assertion of a land without owners, advocated and pursued treaties with the Indigenous peoples.[41] For, a treaty, like a conquest, would have enabled the occupiers to represent the Indigenous will as having been appropriately alienated from its property, (albeit subject to negotiations for compensation). Significantly, from the standpoint of the colonizers a voluntary surrender would have suitably transformed what was recognizably Indigenous property. Alienated land is capable of being possessed; it can receive another will *immediately* (without the need for any further mediation).

For this reason, the failure to give effect to the treaty option and, indeed, the willful perpetuation of the myth of the absence of original owners, did not only deny the Indigenous peoples their subjectivity and sovereignty, they also denied

---

41. Marcia Langton, 'Dominion and Dishonour: A Treaty between our Nations?', *Postcolonial Studies*, vol.4, no.1, pp. 13-26; Henry Reynolds, *Aboriginal Sovereignty*, pp. 108-116.

the occupiers the chance to fulfill the seminal desire of modern Western subjectivity; the colonial will-to-be Australian could not securely ground itself by taking immediate (unmediated) possession of an otherwise will-less thing.

What does this mean for the position of the white occupiers who have seized the land against the Indigenous peoples' resistance? In conformity with the structure of modern Western subjectivity that we outlined earlier, possession must be conceived in terms of the *exclusive* right of the white collective to the whole and entire use of appropriated territory. In the circumstances, to have countenanced the possibility of any part of the land being simultaneously owned by another, would have been to plunge the occupier-will into what Hegel calls an 'insanity of personality'.[42] In this case, the occupier would have been related to the occupied territories as something 'penetrated through and through' by his [or her] own will and 'at the same time there would remain in the thing something impenetrable, namely the will, the empty will of another'.[43] Indigenous survival thus exposes white subjectivity to the *ontological terror* arising from the possibility of 'an insanity of personality' in this sense of threatening the very coherence of a self-grounded or sovereign being as white Australian. In the absence of a successful program of genocide, this situation continues to mark the collective being of white Australia understood as a nation in its becoming.

It comes as no surprise then that in their effort to ground the occupier will-to-be Australian, the occupiers have sought to reconstitute Indigenous land in a *mediated* way. In other words, the land had violently to be emptied of the sovereign will of the Indigenous gathering-we. But Indigenous sovereignty is not reducible to the 'empty will of another'. Michael Dodson explains,

> Our people have left us deep roots, which empowered us to endure the violence of oppression. They are the roots of survival, but not of constriction. They are roots from

---

42. G.W.F. Hegel, *Philosophy of Right*, Remark to § 62, emphasis added.
43. G.W.F. Hegel, *Philosophy of Right*, § 62.

which all growth is possible.
  They are the roots that protected our end from the beginning.[44]

Since modern Western subjectivity requires *unmediated* possession to ground itself securely, this perpetration of violence generates a fundamental disturbance at the level of its ontological structure. This outwardly directed violence corresponds to an inwardly directed self-violation or, what we earlier referred to as an emptying out of the principle of sovereign being. For the gathering-we of the white collective, the process of embodying the will-to-be Australian has accordingly been compromised by the mediating role played by violence.

Moreover, because the ontological disturbance has taken the form of violence, violence has become the effective ground of white Australian being. That is, the violence associated with the murder and forced removal of Indigenous peoples has become a constitutive aspect of what it means for the occupier to be or to become Australian. Indeed, without the perpetuation of this violence white Australia risks being caught up in the problematic of 'the insanity of personality' that we mentioned above. The *Mabo* decision is symptomatic of this very condition. Commenting on the status of the determination from the perspective of international law, Gerry Simpson observes,

> In *Mabo* the Court, having found that Australia was not *terra nullius* [...] invented a completely new category of acquisition—i.e. the occupation of already occupied territory (or occupation of land that is not *terra nullius*. The semantic impossibility of such a finding is matched by its apparent lack of authoritative support in international law.[45]

The 'semantic impossibility of such a finding' underscores the *ontological* impossibility to which the idea of an 'insanity of personality' refers. The Court's insistence on affirming this impossible condition thus perpetuates the violence constitutive of the white Australian being.

---

44. Michael Dodson, 'The End in the Beginning', p. 42.
45. Cited in Gary Foley, 'The Australian Labor Party', p. 132.

What are the implications of this understanding of the constitutive place of violence in the white Australian national imaginary? Firstly, because the violence directed against the Indigenous peoples is the very ground of the occupier's being *as Australian*, being Australian becomes *co-extensive* with the non-recognition of Indigenous peoples as sovereign in their own right. Secondly, since this non-recognition extends to their formal being—to their very being as private property-owning subjects rather than merely to the rights of particular groups over particular portions of land—the land in its totality is implicated in the mediating act of violent dispossession. Australian territory becomes co-extensive with white territory. Through their mediated possession, the occupiers thus give effect to a logic that simultaneously transforms the object of their possession from a particular thing to the whole territory *and* identifies the subject capable of possession with the white property owner. This is how the logic that frames the occupier subject-world relationship renders both Australian subjectivity and Australian territory as exclusively white.

These observations help to explain how the Indigenous peoples' sovereignty has been rendered invisible from the white Australian subject-position. It is as if all inhabitants of Australian/white territory became subject to British Australian colonial authority from the very moment of the latter's inception. From within the limits of this de-historicizing logic it seems meaningless even to raise the question, as does the white historian, of *when*, chronologically speaking, Indigenous sovereignty was supposedly lost.[46]

But the real question concerns, not the loss of Indigenous sovereignty but the failure to respect it and the corresponding masking of the lack of British colonial / white Australian sovereignty. Gary Foley explains,

> Groups such as the Aboriginal Provisional Government (APG) and Melbourne's Black GST argue that if the validity and authority of the High Court were entirely dependent on the myth of *terra nullius*, then did not that

---
46. See Henry Reynolds, *Aboriginal Sovereignty*.

authority and validity instantly cease to exist at the moment it declared *terra nullius* invalid? If Aboriginal sovereignty prevailed, then from the moment it declared *terra nullius* null and void, the High Court had no authority to make any further pronouncements on the issue. The Australian government should then have been required to negotiate with Aboriginal representatives on issues of sovereignty and meaningful compensation instead of imposing the manifestly inferior proposition of 'native title'.

[...] for many Indigenous people there remains a significant question mark over the actual acquisition of sovereignty by the British. It is expected that Indigenous groups will continue to challenge and resist Australian governments on this issue for many years to come.[47]

As the *Mabo* judgment shows, the logic we have been describing continues to inform our ways of being as white Australians to the present day. In its futile efforts to restore the moment of immediacy in the nation-building processes of becoming Australian, white Australia perpetuates the conditions of the ontological disturbance we have sketched. Indeed, in persisting with the active whitening of everything worthy of the name 'Australian', white Australia lives out what we call a self-generated *onto-pathology*. This pathological condition at the ontological level conforms to what Hegel, in a different context, defines as the 'criminal will'.[48] For Hegel, criminality is a form of colonizing activity involving a willful misrepresentation of something particular as universal. In our context, the imperative of whiteness—'act as if the land were initially without owners'—is just such a particular since it is willfully misrepresented as the universal form of the fundamental subject-world relation of private property-owning being that grounds the collective being as Australian. White Australia's onto-pathology conforms to the structure of a *collective criminal will* in so far as its self-instituting practices, most notably in the political and legal systems, are informed by an on-going investment in the imperative of whiteness; the occupiers'

---

47. Gary Foley, 'The Australian Labor Party', p. 133.
48. G.W.F. Hegel, *Philosophy of Right*, § 82-103.

practice of insisting that to be Australian is to respond to the command to be-as-a-world through adherence to the imperative of whiteness.

Are we exaggerating in claiming that the fundamental legal and political institutions of white Australia are premised on the perpetuation of a *willful misrepresentation* characteristic of *collective criminality*? After all, the High Court recognized 'native title' in the common law of Australia and this was formalized when the Keating Labor government passed the *Native Title Act* (1933). On the contrary, in the wake of the Labor government's abandonment of a pledge to deliver national land rights legislation that would enable Aboriginal people to assert their rights as traditional owners and claim land as inalienable freehold title, the *Native Title Act* constitutes *the formal embodiment* of white Australia's collective criminal will. This is evidenced in the government's manipulation of the consultative process leading up to its enactment and, in particular, its refusal to heed 'extensive Indigenous community concern'.[49] Regarding the terms of the legislation, Gary Foley explains,

> While it was said that native title could coexist with other interests, one of the ways it could be 'extinguished' was by 'compulsory acquisition by the Crown'. What a remarkable coincidence that, since 1788, actions by the British, state, territory and Commonwealth governments have 'extinguished' native title in all the prime-land, settled areas of Australia. This extinguishment is without a single cent of compensation payable, despite the fact that vast wealth has been taken from the lands in question over the past 200 years.
>
> [...]
>
> Thus the vast majority of Aboriginal people in Australia are now formally deemed to have been dispossessed without possibility of compensation. And all of this has been achieved by the judiciary and government, conveniently without having to address the primary underlying issue of Indigenous sovereignty.

---

49. Gary Foley, 'The Australian Labor Party', p. 137. Foley gives a detailed account of this process at pp. 134-139.

[...]
> to defend native title is to defend the *fait accompli* of the most extensive single act of dispossession since 1788, and to further impose colonial 'solutions' on Indigenous people.[50]

This willful deployment of the imperative of whiteness at the level of collectively instituting the state underpins white race privilege and through it the process of occupation continues to generate the sense of the collective that is presupposed for (white) nationhood. Indeed, the perpetuation of white race privilege by a society that affirms the notions of equality and a fair go as *national ideals* depends upon a collective ability to exercise a high level of willful blindness to the conflation of Australianness with whiteness that we have sketched above. This is the on-going work of a collective criminal will that defines the white Australian national imaginary. It is at the heart of widespread unwillingness to countenance the idea of a white occupation of the lands of the sovereign Indigenous peoples and it manifests as an on-going anxiety about our connections to stolen land. In the words of Philip Falk and Gary Martin,

> it is the very denial of Indigenous sovereignty that is unsettling the nation, and [...] this unsettling will continue whilst it remains a contentious issue.[51]

White Australians typically insist on needing to know more about the Indigenous other. But from the position we have been elaborating and attributing to white Australia, knowledge of the specifics of the other's world is not necessary for full and proper recognition of the other. Because it places priority on the epistemic standpoint of recognizing the sovereign being of a gathering-we, understanding the complex of meanings that any particular gathering establishes for itself is neither a pre-condition nor even a necessary element of recognition. Rather this sort of understanding typically *flows from* mutual recognition. This is why at the ontological level becoming familiar with and accepting

---

50. Gary Foley, 'The Australian Labor Party', pp. 138-139.
51. Phillip Falk and Gary Martin, 'Misconstruing Indigenous Sovereignty', p. 35.

Indigenous ways cannot be a pre-condition for recognition. Instead white Australia must look to what is fundamental in the encounter, namely Indigenous sovereignty.

What then of the source of the white Australian desire to understand Aboriginal Australians, even to the point of their 'being cannibalized and utilized to Aboriginalize the majority', as Irene Watson observes.[52] One could of course insist on explaining the depths of this epistemological drive by reference to our longstanding European racist sentiments. But if the source of this white Australian desire to understand is indeed the criminality that initially manifests as theft of the land and then proceeds as the ongoing willingness to annihilate all signs of the Indigenous sovereign gathering-we, then it must also be the case that this criminality itself shapes the racism informing white Australia and not the reverse. Let us proceed next to investigate the implications of this order of explanation.

---

52. Irene Watson, 'Settled and Unsettled Spaces', pp. 18-19.

9. RACIST EPISTEMOLOGIES OF A COLLECTIVE CRIMINAL WILL

We have suggested that the collective criminal will of white Australia underpins our racism and not the reverse. We do not mean to deny that racist epistemologies served as the white occupiers' ideological guide from the moment of arrival on the black continent. The point is rather that such ideologies had to be re-shaped and adapted to service *the masking* of white Australia's collective criminal will. In this case, racist epistemologies are not the cause but the symptom of the white Australian onto-pathology. By 'racist epistemologies' we are referring here, both to the many white discourses that 'Aboriginalize' the Indigenous other in the sense of discursively constructing a limited view of the Aborigine, and to the discourses that 'fail to recognize whiteness as a racial category', as Aileen Moreton-Robinson illustrates in relation to the self-professed post-colonial discourses of race. In the latter case,

> Race is implicit in the construct Aborigine but not identified as being implicit in the category European Australian. [...] This ensures that race continues to belong to the Indigenous other and whiteness remains hidden.[53]

For Moreton-Robinson, this is because

> whiteness [has] assumed the status of an epistemological *a priori* in the development of knowledge in modernity

---

53. Aileen Moreton-Robinson, 'Whiteness, Epistemology and Indigenous Representation', p. 82.

> [...]. Whiteness as an epistemological *a priori* provides
> a way of knowing and being that is predicated on su-
> periority, which becomes normalized and forms part of
> one's taken-for granted-knowledge.[54]

Our claim is that the white Australian ways of knowing, and hence the ways of knowing the Indigenous other, which have developed as the failure to recognize Indigenous sovereignty, spring directly from the depths of white Australia's unwillingness to confront our onto-pathology. This tight connection between the white Australian collective criminal will and its racist epistemologies is evident when we focus on the white nation's occupier being *as a whole*, a being that, as we suggested earlier, is directed to the annihilation of Indigenous sovereign being by targeting both the bearer of the question 'where do you come from?' as well as the question itself. We want to suggest that the logic underpinning the perpetual enactment of our onto-pathology leads the white Australian collective criminal will to manifest its *negative* self-affirmation through a triple act of displacing, claiming and denying. The result of this process is an erasure from white Australian memory of the mediating role of violence, which opens up the conceptual space for white Australia's now *positive* self-affirmation. Let us consider these moves in turn.

Firstly, that whiteness functions as an epistemological *a priori* in the abovementioned way or, in other words, that we are knowing subjects in so far as we take for granted our whiteness, presupposes that we do not take ourselves to be unknowing as regards our own origins. That is we must *already know* where we come from (in the ontological sense explained earlier of naming and accounting for our being) if we are reflectively to relate to the world through our taken-for-granted whiteness. So this reflective standpoint presupposes that the question of our origins has already been eliminated from our view. For the white Australian knower then *there is no question of our origins*. Our desire for knowing

---

54. Aileen Moreton-Robinson, 'Whiteness, Epistemology and Indigenous Representation', p. 75-76.

can therefore be meaningfully directed outwardly, that is, to those who are not like us and to an account of *their* being or non-being. This makes sense of Michael Dodson's observation that

> Constant proclamations that Indigenous peoples are remnants of a past doomed to extinction, that 'the old Aboriginal world is now facing its final twilight' and that Aboriginal people are 'powerless to defend themselves against the final onslaught' continue to construct us as innately obsolete people.[55]

Moreover, the act of displacing the Aboriginal other generates an infinite distance between the (white) knowing subject and the Indigenous other, a distance that the knowing subject perpetually aspires to traverse. Again as Dodson sums up,

> To the early visitors we varied from the noble savage to the prehistoric beast. [...]
>
> In the law we were defined systematically, though variably, according to proportions of black blood. [...]
>
> Their men of religion were also concerned to define us [as "degraded as to divine things" and "lost to all moral and spirit perception".]
>
> Their hopeful educators assessed our capacity for learning. On the one hand, they were certain of our inherent handicaps and defects [... as] "lacking in reflection, judgment and foresight"]. On the other, we represented a potential for manipulation [... "as capable of instruction as any other untutored savages" ...]
>
> Their men of science believed they could locate the definitive answers in our brains and blood. [...]
>
> And we have been an ever-popular subject for portrayal in paintings or films. Initially, we appeared as the noble well-built native: heroic, bearded, loin-clothed, one foot up, vigilant and boomerang at the ready. Later, after we had fallen from grace, we appeared bent, distorted, overweight, inebriated, with bottle in hand. And more recently, we appear ochred, spiritual and playing the didjeridu behind the heroic travels of a black Landcruiser.

---

55. Michael Dodson, 'The End in the Beginning', p. 28.

> [...]
> Since their first intrusive gaze, colonizing cultures have had a preoccupation with observing, analyzing, studying, classifying and labeling Aborigines and Aboriginality. Under that gaze, Aboriginality changed from being a daily practice to being 'a problem to be solved'.[56]

The act of claiming the other takes place through the objectification of the Aborigine. Represented as lacking the power of self-knowledge and indeed the power to know more generally, Indigenous Australians appear as the mere objects of reflection of the white gaze. Here the occupier's denial of Indigenous sovereignty manifests through the act of claiming Aboriginality as the object that *is* only in so far as it is accessible to the occupier's knowing. This strategy of reducing the other to *the known* generates the appearance of an 'innocent' desire on the part of the occupier to epistemically appropriate the Indigenous other. The production of white innocence constitutes the moment of claiming the exclusive power of definition.

This perpetual claiming of the power to know, through the enforcement of the premise, 'you do not know', excludes or trivializes Indigenous knowledges. As Aileen Moreton-Robinson observes, through the process of objectification

> [t]he knowledges we have developed are often dismissed as being implausible, subjective, or lacking in epistemological integrity.[57]

But the reduction of the Indigenous other to the known, and hence the *non-knowing* other, also eliminates the bearer of the question of origins from the white knower's field of vision. This constitutes an epistemological transformation of the being of the occupier through the elimination of Indigenous ontological sovereignty from the field of vision of the (white) knower. Thus the white subject's experience of epistemological innocence conceals the ontological wish to deny our onto-pathology even as we enact it.

---

56. Michael Dodson, 'The End in the Beginning', pp. 26-27.

57. Aileen Moreton-Robinson, 'Whiteness, Epistemology and Indigenous Representation', p. 85.

Moreover, the abovementioned act of claiming (the exclusive power to know the Indigenous other as the merely known) also enables the premise 'you *cannot* know' to serve as the taken-for-granted starting point of white knowledge claims. As Lester-Irabinna Rigney explains,

> [i]f we recognize that Australian science is racialized, we must also recognize that non-Indigenous Australians alike have learnt to devalue and give little recognition to Indigenous contributions, intellects and cultures. Whilst the construct of 'race' informs and legitimates '*terra nullius*', it also informs the assumption by colonists and subsequent generations that Indigenous traditions of intelligentsia equate to '*Intellectual Nullius*'.[58]

And as Michael Dodson explains, because 'our voices and our visions have been notably absent',

> today, to even begin to speak about Aboriginality is to enter a labyrinth full of obscure passages, ambiguous signs and trapdoors. The moment the question is asked, 'Who or what is Aboriginal?' an historical landscape is entered, full of absolute and timeless truths, which have been set in place by self-professed experts and authorities all too ready to tell us, and the world, the meaning of Aboriginality.[59]

In order to function at all, white epistemologies must therefore be capable of removing from the white cognitive field the very pre-condition of the whiteness of their knowing—that is, of knowing in accordance with the imperative of whiteness, to act as if the land were initially without owners—namely the criminality at the heart of the white Australian collective will. This is why the Indigenous other must be both ontologically *and epistemologically* displaced and claimed in such a way as to simultaneously hide the displacing as well as the reason for it. This act of denial is co-extensive with a *willful* blindness to the effects of our being as white Australian, to the question of our origins and to the bearer of the question as a sovereign being. We are

---

58. Lester-Irabinna Rigney, 'A First Perspective of Indigenous Australian Participation in Science', p. 4.

59. Michael Dodson, 'The End in the Beginning', p. 28.

uncomfortably reminded of this with every act of Indigenous resistance. As Tracey Bunda explains,

> Our knowing of ourselves is always in contrast to the colonisers' representations of who we are.[60]

For Bunda, black women's voices of resistance 'affirm our being in sovereignty', in opposition to the colonisers' practice of constructing and therefore knowing and owning the subject.[61] For Lester-Irabinna Rigney, it is 'Indigenist research' that produces genuine knowledge of the Indigenous ontological reality:

> Indigenist research [...] offers a strategy for Indigenous research by Indigenous peoples for Indigenous peoples and in the interests of Indigenous peoples. Indigenist Research offers three core, interrelated principles: Resistance (as the emancipatory imperative); political integrity; and privileging Aboriginal and Torres Strait Islander voices.[62]

In this way the white epistemological plane of objectification becomes the site of the ontological intensification of the sovereignty of the Indigenous resisting subject. From the reflective standpoint of whiteness whose displacing act eliminates Indigenous sovereignty from view, enabling the reduction of Indigeneity to an object to be epistemically claimed, this sovereignty has no place given the imperative of whiteness. It therefore functions as an interiority that perpetually irrupts into the exterior white spaces in a continuous and defiant assertion of self-determination, which in posing the question, 'where do you come from?', exposes the failure in the abovementioned eliminationist and reductionist epistemological strategies of the imperative of whiteness.

The deployment of such eliminationist and reductionist strategies marks the early and post-Federation phases of the occupation in which the exclusion of the Indigenous other from the ontological plane of white nation-building was premised on the epistemological principle that asserts

---

60. Tracey Bunda, 'The Sovereign Aboriginal Woman', p. 75.

61. Tracey Bunda, 'The Sovereign Aboriginal Woman', p. 76.

62. Lester-Irabinna Rigney, 'A First Perspective of Indigenous Australian Participation in Science', p. 8.

an unbridgeable gap between Indigeneity and sovereignty. Precisely because the white Australian collective willfully denies the sovereign being of the original owners, the meaning of Indigenous resistance, sacrifice and survival becomes crucial. In the words of Michael Dodson,

> Nearly suffocated with imposed labels and structures, Aboriginal people have had no other choice than to insist on our right to speak back, to do as the old man said: to build and represent our own world of meaning and significance.[63]

Ironically, actions that in different circumstances would have been considered evidence of supreme acts of ontological sovereignty are epistemically transformed into the actions, at best, of ignorant nuisances who must be disciplined and, at worst, of pests that must be eliminated lest we hear the response to the question of our origins, 'you are the occupiers'. In the words of Aileen Moreton-Robinson,

> The very existence of white women and men is thus a constant reminder that our lands were invaded and stolen, our ancestors massacred and enslaved, our children taken and our rights denied and that these acts of terror forged white identity in this country. The presence of white bodies is connected to invasion, theft, murder and domination. White corporeality is thus one of the myriad ways in which relations between the colonizing past and present are omnipresent.[64]

As we have seen, in all the abovementioned constructions of Aboriginality, whiteness and their interplay, racism serves to satisfy the epistemological needs that the ontology of the collective criminal will generates throughout the early and post-Federation phases of the occupation. By displacing the other the occupier claims the exclusive power to define the other's identity and this also has the effect of eliminating the other's sovereign being from the white knower's

---

63. Michael Dodson, 'The End in the Beginning', p. 28.
64. Aileen Moreton-Robinson, 'Tiddas Talkin' Up to the White Woman: When Huggins et. al. Took on Bell' in Michelle Grossman (ed.), *Blacklines: Contemporary Critical Writing by Indigenous Australians*, Melbourne, Melbourne University Press, 2003, pp. 66-77, p. 67.

gaze. Still the denial of Indigenous sovereignty does not erase the effects of the white Australian onto-pathology. The Indigenous other is therefore also constructed as 'material' suited to a more positive epistemological reformulation. Let us explain.

With Federation and the instituted whitening of the land as a whole white Australia enacts the imperative of whiteness *as a nation*, thereby feigning *immediate* (unmediated) possession of the land in its totality. Post-Federation Indigenous Australians no longer signify the threat of territorial boundaries for white Australia. The hypothetical nation has emerged historically and announced itself to its proud people as well as to the rest of the world. Yet, the ever-present logic of criminality drives the occupier to see, not just the immigrants, but *everyone* who is not part of the self-instituting white gathering-we as coming into its sovereign space *from the outside,* so to speak. Such an ontological reception entails that only the white collective can claim genuine sovereignty and only the white nation can determine the conditions of inclusion of others in this sovereign being. Here we can sense how deeply rooted in the ontological history of the criminal will was John Howard's insistence that 'we' (white Australians) decide who can come to this country.[65]

This means that Indigenous Australians must *become* Australian, *like the immigrants*. In claiming 'we are one [...] we are Australian' white Australia at once conflates the ontology of whiteness with knowledge of the question of origins—we know where we come from—and establishes the dependence of the conditions of Indigenous sovereign / Australian being on an epistemological formulation of the terms of access to whiteness. (You are *like us.*) In the words of Ian Anderson,

> To be an Australian citizen, for a person of Aboriginal heritage, meant nothing less than becoming a white Australian with a black skin.[66]

---

65. See Toula Nicolacopoulos and George Vassilacopoulos, 'Rethinking the Radical Potential of the Concept of Multiculturalism'.

66. Ian Anderson, 'Black Bit, White Bit', in Michelle Grossman (ed.), *Blacklines: Contemporary Critical Writing by Indigenous Australians*,

Here the epistemology of exclusion of the Indigenous other has been replaced by the epistemology of including Indigenous Australians on the ontological plane of white sovereignty.

White Australia's insistence on actively whitening the Indigenous other must be ongoing given that, due to the very meaning of sovereignty as *self*-determination, the erasing of Indigenous sovereignty remains a perpetually unfinished project.

For this reason white Australia constructs the Indigene as a white subject through a double abstraction. Having epistemically abstracted the Indigenous peoples from their ontological sovereignty (having rendered Indigenous sovereignty invisible to the white knower's gaze), white Australia simultaneously precludes their full immersion in the sovereign spaces of the white collective. This is because in order to become white Indigenous Australians are expected to forget that they are the sovereign owners of this land. But since the requisite act of forgetting is mediated by the imperative of whiteness, which fabricates the 'memory' of exclusive ownership as integral to the self-instituting being of the white collective, forgetting is not like cutting off certain ties once and for all as the precondition for becoming white. Instead Indigenous Australians are called upon specifically to enact whiteness as *the practice of forgetting*, that is, as the reverse of the positive remembering of exclusive ownership that defines white Australia. Indigenous Australians are thus suspended in the epistemological spaces that the white collective perpetually creates for them in order to accept them conditionally into the white collective. The hypothetical nation thus treats the other as if he / she were white transforming the Indigenous other into *the virtual white* subject. Epistemology grounded on the denial of Indigenous ontological sovereignty thus creates virtual white subjects in spaces where *to be is to be known by the white institutions* in ways that affirm this knowing by hiding the ontological dimension of the white Australian collective criminal will, which is the *topos* from which the white institutions perpetually spring. White Australia thus creates the Indigene as a legal and political subject with rights. But since such creation is mediated by the dispossession and corresponding denial of the ontological right to be, the Indigene is only *epistemically* (known as) a subject with legal/political rights. The Indigenous other thus remains an object whilst simultaneously being made into a subject. The very same eliminationist and reductionist epistemological strategies that bring about the displacing, claiming and denying of Indigeneity, continue to function alongside the expectation that Indigenous Australians become white.

Having been abstracted from the sovereign right to be in one's own terms and having been abstractly constructed into virtual whites, what is left for Indigenous Australians? Indigeneity must be constructed as an ethnicity, which as we suggested earlier, places Indigeneity on a par with the ethnicities of non-British migrants. Ultimately the legal and political rights assigned to the Indigenous Australians do not mirror the rights of recognition due to sovereign peoples. They are the rights of ethnicity, of cultural difference and so on. Such rights presuppose the ontological differentiation between the right-conferring sovereign white gathering and all others. Land rights are thus effectively reduced to identity rights. In this context Indigenous Australians are perpetually asked to prove the continuity of their identity in abstraction from the continuity of their ontological sovereignty. Given that Indigenous Australians are constructed as virtual white subjects and hence are not recognized as sovereign owners in their own right they are always called upon to prove their claims to own their lands. But because qua virtual whites, Indigenous Australians emerge in the epistemological spaces created for them as a result of the onto-pathology of the white collective, the relation between Indigeneity and ownership of the land is constantly open to interpretations serving the interests of white Australia. The authorities of whiteness elevate themselves to the position of protector of the institutions and the cohesiveness of (white) society as a whole against false claims of property ownership. This is why control over specification of the formal criteria for determining the authenticity or otherwise of identity and associated rights claims is so important.

Thus paradoxically even in denying the existence of the white Australian collective criminal will, these racist epistemologies ultimately serve to intensify the criminality that is at the heart of white Australian being and the corresponding resisting sovereignty that is the impenetrable core of Indigenous Australian being.

10. THE PERPETUAL-FOREIGNER-WITHIN AS AN EPISTEMOLOGICAL CONSTRUCTION

We have been arguing that in calling upon Indigenous Australians to forget their sovereign being as a pre-condition for being recognized as knowing subjects, white Australia reduces Indigenous Australians to 'virtual whites'. This is one of the effects of the white Australian onto-pathology and, in particular, of its outwardly directed violence. We have also seen that the dispossession of the Indigenous peoples has had the further unintended effect of violating the fundamental structure of the property-owning identity that is at the heart of white Australian being. That is, white Australia—the members of the white collective, the state and its institutions—does not simply lack ontological sovereignty and genuine ownership over the land. Rather, having sunk into the darkness of the 'insanity of personality'—the problematic condition of seeking to embody one's will exclusively in some thing that is already an embodied being—white Australia now deploys its collective criminal will, thus perpetuating a problematic anxiety-producing condition. All this is tied to the survival and ongoing resistance of the Indigenous peoples who refuse to set aside the issue of white Australia's lack of authority and genuine ownership of the land.

Under these conditions white Australia cannot reconcile its being with the land in an ontologically appropriate manner. Our onto-pathology thus generates an ongoing desire to 'restore' the ontological balance, the integrity of the white Australian collective as mutually respectful persons who recognize each others' property-owning being, without however facing up to the realities of the constitutive role that outwardly directed violence and inwardly directed violation have played in the formation of our being. In the absence of such 'restorative work' white Australia would be overwhelmed by the criminality and the 'insanity of personality' that define and permeate our being as a collective.

Accordingly, the white Australian national imaginary has produced a story through which to 'restore' the ontological balance of white Australian being and to alleviate the anxiety associated with its onto-pathological condition. This is the story of 'the perpetual-foreigner-within', an epistemological construction aimed at satisfying the demands for ontological recognition in the absence of which white Australia cannot function, since, for the modern Western property-owning ontology property owners' mutual recognition is indispensable to the fundamental structure of relations. How must this story unfold if it is to serve the needs of white Australia's onto-pathology effectively? Why must it be the perpetual-foreigner-within who recognizes white Australian property-owning authority and who can play such a role?

To begin with, recognition must come from a suitable other and this other of the white Australian cannot be the Indigene since, as we have already seen, this latter is denied the very capacity to take part in the mutual recognition of property-owning beings. Nor can the other be an external power, as in the case of sovereign states recognizing one another in international relations. Such recognition from the outside, so to speak, is inadequate for two reasons. Firstly, the mutual recognition of sovereign states is always contingent and strategic in its orientation since it is grounded in the respective interests of the parties already operating in the international arena. Secondly, and more to the point, such recognition presupposes that the collective body whose sovereignty is being recognised by another state already recognizes its own being as sovereign. But the issue for white Australia concerns the very act of the originating self-institution of the collective as a gathering-we, not other states' recognition of that which flows from such legitimate self-institution, namely the white Australian nation-state. It is sovereignty in this internal sense, which is linked to the performance of the very act of becoming a sovereign being, to which the restoration of balance must be directed since this is the source of the onto-pathology. In order to be effective, then, the source of the requisite recognition must be capable of playing an integral part in the story of the sovereign self-instituting being of the white Australian collective.

More specifically, given that the source of the ontological problem is the inability to take immediate (unmediated) possession of the land, it is the absence of this element of immediacy that must be redressed. But since it is not possible to secure unmediated possession in the light of Indigenous survival, the restorative work can only be directed to the *representation* of possession as unmediated. In these circumstances an implicit denial of Indigenous sovereignty by a suitable other corresponds to an affirmation of white Australia's self-presentation as having taken immediate possession of the land. White Australia is in a position to redirect its attention away from its criminality and towards the appearance of ontologically legitimate possession only by co-opting an other who is capable of taking part in the processes of recognition that underpin the act of taking possession of the land as an originating act of the collective. Thus in the very act of (re)positioning ourselves towards Australian territory as rightful owners, the white Australian occupiers must at once perpetually redirect attention away from the absence of the ontological act of immediate possession that ought to have underpinned this claim to ownership, and towards one who is positioned to offer the appropriate recognition. Here there is a shift of attention from the immediacy concerning the way in which the occupier acts upon the thing to the question of how the act of possession is received. The other must therefore be positioned to recognize white Australians as the sovereign owners who are immediately related to the land of Australia.

Accordingly, the restorative work in question operates only at the epistemological level. That is, it affects the question of how white Australia presents itself and how this self-presentation must be received. The restorative work cannot address the question of how white Australia *is* in relation to the land given that Indigenous dispossession has given rise to a white Australian collective that, as we suggested, has lost the integrity of its being, its ontological power for sovereign self-institution through immediate possession of the land. So it can never have a transformative impact at the ontological level. Having lost *the grounding* of the very idea of self-institution—though not the cultural investment in conforming to the idea of a self-instituting gathering-we—white Australian being must 'flood' the emptiness created by its self-inflicted loss with a knowing relation that enables white Australia to present its sovereignty, all the while keeping the ontological roots of this situation hidden.

What form must the requisite knowing relation take between the white Australian occupier and the other in order that the latter be positioned to give the requisite recognition? Since it is the unmediated possession of the land that must remain hidden, the white knower cannot say 'the land is mine, therefore, it is not yours', as do the genuine owners, the Indigenous peoples, to the white occupiers. (The assertion 'is mine' must always be absolutely grounded in immediate possession, which in the case of the occupier has been violated.) The only option available to the white Australian occupier is to say, 'the land is not yours, therefore, it is mine.' Here, the occupier makes the assertion, 'it is mine', through the mediation of the claim, 'it is not yours'. In this way, the element of immediacy that ought to determine the correctness of 'it is mine' is itself covered over by the initial negative assertion. The very form of the abovementioned knowing relation in turn determines the representation of the mode of being of the other who can at once affirm the correctness of the assertion and recognize white Australian sovereign being. Here the demand for immediate possession dictates that time, the time of arrival, is the determining factor.

The white Australian collective generates the 'memory' of rightful ownership and sovereign being by presenting to an other as *always having been here* if and only if the other arrives on the scene *after* the white Australian collective. To be positioned to act as the genuine receiver of the words 'the land is not yours' the relevant other must therefore be the foreigner. It is in the presence of the foreigner that I can recall and present myself as the sovereign creator of the white Australian nation-state. This is where our onto-pathology gives rise to a tension that determines the precise qualities that the foreigner must embody. For the reasons already explained, on the one hand, the genuine (re)enactment of sovereignty cannot be mediated by something external to the self-instituting collective and, on the other, white Australia depends upon just this sort of recognition from the outside, so to speak, in so far as it relies on the foreigner. Hence, in order to restore integrity to the enactment of sovereignty those with the potential to offer the requisite recognition must be able themselves to participate in the act at the same time as being positioned outside of it. This is the role that must be performed by the foreigner-within. The foreigner-within is simultaneously positioned as inside and outside the white Australian collective by combining a white insider property-owning identity, which constitutes the foreigner as an individual subject, with a non-white outsider difference that constitutes the foreigner as a member of a racialized collective. The white Australian collective is thus divided into a dominant group, the ones in need of recognition, and the foreigners-within who would-be white Australian.

In a desperate attempt to exorcise its collective criminal will, since Federation white Australia has managed the ongoing processes that define the foreigner as the foreigner-within. Firstly, the foreigners are allowed into the country in so far as we conform our identity to that of a private property-owning subjectivity with the potential to be fully implicated in the social network of commodity circulation. That is, our value is measured by our potential for involvement in production and consumption through our wealth and/or alienation of our labour power. In thus recognizing the foreigner-within as a formal subject, dominant white Australia qualifies the foreigner-within to participate in the processes of mutual recognition through which white Australia can claim rightful ownership of the country. In turn, by recognizing white Australian authority, the foreigner-within becomes fully complicit in the on-going violent dispossession of the Indigenous peoples and the nation building processes that manifest our collective criminal will. The foreigners who are thus welcomed into the country share with the dominant white Australian subject position the characteristic of taking for granted our own whiteness—the imperative to act as if the land were without the Indigenous owners—and/or rendering invisible our access to white race privileges. This makes the foreigners-within doubly complicit in the dispossession of the Indigenous peoples, irrespective of whether or not we endorse anti-racism. As Jane Haggis has urged, it is a serious mistake to imply that anti-racists somehow occupy a moral space of no or less complicity.[67]

Secondly, because recognition from the foreigner-within serves the role of relieving the anxiety of the white Australian nation's criminally constituted will, white Australia's authority to control national territorial borders is an indispensable, though not sufficient, part of this recognition. It is not just the unwelcome foreigners who are constituted as perpetual foreigners. On the contrary, the foreigners-within must be constituted as *perpetual* foreigners irrespective of whether or not they are recognized as white property-owning insiders. This is because the foreigner-within who is positioned to give recognition must also *remain distinguishable* from the dominant white Australian. The white anxiety that derives from the criminality harboured in the national imaginary needs the foreigner to remain *forever* dependent on the dominant white Australians who grant us permission, not only

---

67. Jane Haggis, 'Beyond Race and Whiteness? Reflections on the New Abolitionists and an Australian Critical Whiteness Studies', *borderlands e-journal*, 2004, www.borderlandsejournal.adelaide.edu.au/vol-3no2_2004/haggis_beyond.htm .

to enter the country but to stay on. Against the background of the onto-pathology we have described, an affirmation of the legitimacy of the dominant white Australian culture and of the authority of its state depend on the perpetuation of just this sort of relationship of mutual dependence.

11. THE MIGRANT AS WHITE-NON-WHITE AND WHITE-BUT-NOT-WHITE-ENOUGH

We have suggested that dominant white Australia invokes the perpetual-foreigner-within since it must continuously posit a suitable other through whom to claim rightful control of Australian territory at the same time as alleviating the anxiety generated by the white Australian collective criminal will. This epistemological construction of the white property-owning insider who is at once the non-white outsider is potentially embodied as the migrant / refugee who is welcomed into the country. That is, a certain category of (im)migrant is positioned to give and receive the necessary form of mutual recognition whilst remaining readily visible as a foreigner. Indeed the white Australian onto-pathology and consequent dependence on a perpetual-foreigner-within provide the key to understanding how the institutions of dominant white Australia ambiguously position certain migrant and ethnic groups who fall within the control of the white Australian state. Although migrancy forms part of the history of all non-Indigenous Australians, dominant white Australia does not typically identify with the categories of the immigrant, the migrant or the ethnic. Instead, a presumptive association of migrancy with some racialized element(s) epistemologically reinforces the association of migrancy with foreigner-being and the corresponding ontological illusion that the members of the white Australian collective have somehow always already been here. The categories, migrant and immigrant, are thus reserved for 'later arrivals', although length of personal or ancestral stay in Australia does not determine inclusion in them.

Dominant white Australia thus positions designated migrant and ethnic minority groups as social inside-outsiders. It does this by reference to the interplay of their members' dual identity as private property-owning subjects (white insiders) and as bearers of a racialized difference (non-white outsiders). Whereas in their capacity as property-owning subjects the members of such groups are *like* the dominant Europeans/Anglophones of white Australia, they nevertheless always remain distinguishable from them by reference to their residual racialized differences. Here, the markers of racialized difference need not consist of a set of fixed essential characteristics, like 'skin colour' or 'racial affiliation', but may instead be drawn from any number of assigned group characteristics that can be relied upon to render visible the members of a designated group. Indeed the visibility of any group that suitably marks it as a perpetual-foreigner group is not a pre-given state of affairs. Instead it results from the assignment process that meets the needs of dominant white Australia in the light of contingent historical associations between a whiteness that, as Jon Stratton explains, 'equates with assumptions about the phenotypical characteristics of people from northern Europe' and various elements of culture, such as religious affiliation. So, for example, 'where Christianity reinforces whiteness, those who are identified as non-white have that identification reinforced if they also profess a faith other than Christianity'.[68]

The special quality of the social groups positioned as such inside-outsiders is that their individual members can *remain* perpetual foreigners irrespective of their particular histories and characteristics—such as formal citizenship status, place of birth, length of stay in the country and so on. From the standpoint of the dominant white Australian, the perpetual-foreigner-within is at best *like us* in aspiring

---

68. Jon Stratton, *Uncertain Lives: Culture, Race and Neoliberalism in Australia*, Newcastle upon Tyne, UK, Cambridge Scholars Publishing, 2011, pp. 5-9.

to the benefits of Australian citizenship but *unlike us* in that he or she can claim no right to such benefits. The members of groups assigned the identity and role of perpetual-foreigners-within have the status to engage in the processes of recognition that bind the foreigners-within to their white Australian 'hosts' and directly implicate the former in the latter's denial of Indigenous sovereignty rights.

Historically, the notion of the perpetual-foreigner-within has operated as a migrant and ethnic minority discourse as well as cutting across and informing official and public understandings of the social status of various (im)migrant groups. It also operates through a range of Anglophone discourses of the foreigner beyond official policy and political speeches. The media and intelligence services, the courts, trade unions and representations of public opinion more generally all have had a role to play in perpetuating foreigner discourses in relation to the legal, political, economic and social status of immigrants.[69]

Sometimes there is explicit mention of 'the foreigners' but more often the notion of the perpetual-foreigner-within operates covertly to frame and influence what comes to be seen as appropriate treatment of the classes of people who happen to fall within its scope at the particular historical moment. For example, prior to official multiculturalism the Anglophone foreigner discourses invoked a racialized ethnic difference to position Southern European communities as non-white. With Australia's transition to official multiculturalism, and the consequent redefinition of migrant communities as ethnic communities, the legitimating and

---

69. For further discussion of the perpetual-foreigner-within as a migrant and ethnic minority discourse see Toula Nicolacopoulos and George Vassilacopoulos, 'The Making of Greek-Australian Citizenship: From Heteronomous to Autonomous Political Communities', *Journal of Modern Greek Studies* vol.11/12, 2003/4, pp. 165-176. For elaboration of the history of Anglophone Australian Southern European foreigner discourses see Toula Nicolacopoulos and George Vassilacopoulos, 'Discursive Constructions of the Southern European Foreigner', in Ben Wadham and Suzanne Scheck (eds.), *Placing Race and Localising Whiteness Conference Proceedings*, Adelaide, Flinders University Press, 2004, pp. 73-81.

anxiety-relieving role of 'foreigner communities' has been reassigned. The foreigner communities are now more readily positioned in the spaces made available to the detention centre asylum seekers. But white Australia's reception of the latter bears some remarkable similarities with the treatment of Southern European migrant communities of earlier times. Today, Southern Europeans are more often positioned as white-but-not-white-enough. This marks the residual racialized difference that must always distinguish us if we are to play our anxiety-relieving role and the gesture reminds us of the fundamental reason for our being tolerated in the spaces inhabited by the dominant white Australian culture. We are here to serve the very specific and indispensable role of supplying the recognition that ought to have been given to and received from the Indigenous peoples. Indeed, this latter cannot be given and received in the absence of recognition of the Indigenous peoples' sovereignty, a form of recognition that would effectively require elimination of the dominance of white Australian institutions and culture.

12. THREE IMAGES OF THE FOREIGNER-WITHIN: SUBVERSIVE, COMPLIANT, SUBMISSIVE

The covert operation of the notion of the perpetual-foreigner-within works through the dynamics of three inter-related images of the foreigner that conform to three distinct ways of relating its two defining qualities. One gives priority to the foreigner's racialized difference. Another concentrates on the foreigner's power to exercise his or her private property-owning power. Yet a third way of relating the perpetual foreigner's defining qualities has been to attempt to balance them in some way. Prior to the adoption of the state policy of multiculturalism, the dominant white Australian discourses relied on two images of the foreigner. One was the image of the foreigner as 'subversive' and the other represented the foreigner as potentially 'compliant'. Each had a role to play in transforming the migrant into the perpetual-foreigner-within since together they were responsible for socially instituting the two indispensable qualities. Whereas the subversive foreigner image gave priority to the foreigner's racialized difference as a *group attribute*, the image of the compliant foreigner reinforced the recognition of the foreigner's property-owning identity in his or her capacity as an *individual*.

The key element of the subversive foreigner image is the idea that migrants' political allegiance is dictated by their national origins. It follows from this that all non-British nationals constitute a potential danger to the nation. Here, the actions or omissions of individuals are of no consequence since the image of the foreigner pertains to the group's non-white identity. From this perspective foreigner communities are inherently subversive just in virtue of containing their unassimilable racialized difference. Although their members' potential for danger may or may not manifest in expressions of 'disloyalty' or 'anti-social behaviour' of various forms, for dominant white Australia subversive communities constitute the *visible sites* of unassimilable racialized difference.

By contrast, at the heart of the image of the compliant foreigner is the view that since there is no necessary connection between political allegiance and national origins it is open to *individual (im)migrants* to demonstrate their loyalty to the nation. As individuals, rather than as members of their ethnic communities, migrants are *in principle* assimilable by virtue of the exercise of their private property-owning identities. Behaviourally, they can adopt and adapt to the ways of 'the host' society and thereby demonstrate compliance with the expectations of them. Still because they can never be fully absorbed as a collective, the migrants who are constructed through the image of the compliant foreigner remain *not-white-enough*. It is worth noting here that this image of the compliant foreigner bears some similarity to Jon Stratton's idea of 'honorary whites', which he uses in connection with Australians of Asian and African backgrounds. Stratton explains that 'honorary whiteness' is conditionally conferred on typically well-educated Asian and African Australians who present as assimilated into middle class Australian values and this provides them with an invisibility that protects against race-based exclusions.[70] The compliant foreigner discourse similarly confers the benefits of whiteness *conditionally* upon the foreigner who meets the expectations of dominant white Australia. However, the expectations in question concern matters of political allegiance and, above all, recognition of the white Australian state's authority, rather than middle class values.

So whereas the image of the subversive foreigner involves a total eclipse of the foreigner's whiteness such that

---

70. Jon Stratton, *Uncertain Lives*, pp. 214-221.

group membership unavoidably designates every individual as non-white, the image of the compliant foreigner admits of varying traces of whiteness, though the whiteness in question is never enough for full membership into the dominant white Australian collective where links to racialized migrancy and ethnic communities continue.

The interplay of the images of the subversive and the compliant foreigner provide a framework in which to identify a clear pattern in Australia's treatment of non-British migrants notwithstanding the state's endorsement of multiculturalism since the 1970s. So, for example, today's asylum seekers from the Middle East retain their position as perpetual-foreigners-within in striking similarity to Australia's Southern European immigrants of the 1930s. On the one hand, since Federation the official White Australia policy identified Southern Europeans, unlike other categories of immigrants, as potentially white enough to be naturalized. On the other hand, the Anglophone official and public discourses systematically constructed the Southern European communities as inherently subversive *foreigner communities*. Since official multiculturalism, this sort of treatment has been redirected away from the Southern European communities that have been repositioned as *exemplary ethnic communities* to the asylum seeker communities. So, for example, just as the lawmakers had previously denied legal entitlements to naturalized British subjects of Southern European origins, the Howard government refused to conform its handling of refugees to the United Nations Conventions by which Australia is legally bound. In conformity with the image of the subversive foreigner, the asylum seekers' indefinite confinement to the detention centres, not only while their applications are being assessed, but also potentially for life, becomes part of the reality of white Australia.[71] Similarly, the government policy of refusing to grant asylum seekers any right to work paradigmatically registered white Australia's

---

71. See David Marr, 'Is the Media Asleep?' in Robert Manne (ed.), *Do Not Disturb: Is the Media Failing Australia?*, Melbourne, Black Inc Agenda, 2005, pp. 216-230.

unwillingness to recognize asylum seekers' property-owning subjectivity in much the same way that Australian governments had denied equal treatment before the law to certain classes of immigrants from the 1920s to the 1940s. In the twenty-first century the practice of granting fixed term temporary protection visas to asylum seekers in place of permanent visas bears the very same mark of rendering a certain class of immigrant bodies as potentially available to be singled out for discriminatory treatment by the Australian state as did the association in the 1930s of all non-British born nationals with inherently subversive leftist ideas.

Moreover, in keeping with the dual interplay of the subversive and compliant foreigner images not all asylum seekers are positioned as subversive foreigners. Indeed, the public discourse that praises valid entry visa holders shows that white Australia's multicultural values do not extend, as a matter of principle, to white Australia's reception of refugees and the public acceptance of a policy that would see the government 'settling' refugees to Australia in neighbouring countries now serves to maintain the visibility of the subversive foreigner communities in the context of globalization and the expansion of white Australia's population control in the Asia-Pacific region.

The image of the subversive foreigner dominated across the Anglophone discourses until the early 1940s when the Curtin Labor Government began preparations for the mass migration program. Although the two images operated throughout the 1950s and 1960s, the image of the compliant foreigner came to dominate the Anglophone discourses in this period. So, for example, when in 1966 the Holt Government introduced a parliamentary Bill to conscript non-naturalized migrants for service in the Vietnam war, Prime Minister Holt took the view that new-comers should not be allowed to hide behind the legal technicality of not having been naturalized in order to gain an 'unfair advantage' over the Australian-born youth being conscripted. This view reflected the dominant discourse of the times that demanded from the compliant foreigner that he show his allegiance to the white Australian state and people by conforming to their expectations.

Historically, the Anglophone official and public discourses of the foreigner have not been rigid in their assignment of the various images of the perpetual-foreigner-within to specific migrant and ethnic communities and their individual members. Indeed whenever migrant and ethnic communities have reacted to white Australia's involvement in overseas wars, the official response reflects a shifting, inherently flexible assignment processes. For example, migrants' public opposition to Australia's war involvement served as proof of their status as subversive foreigners. So, for example, when non-British migrants distributed anti-war leaflets in the 1930s the government responded with internment to what it took to be *inherently subversive* acts. By the 1960s, still prior to official multiculturalism, anti-Vietnam war activists risked rejection of their naturalization applications, not because they were identified as belonging to inherently subversive foreigner communities, but because their actions showed them to be failing to conform to the image of the compliant foreigner. Post multiculturalism the significance of migrant groups' opposition to Australia's involvement in overseas wars has changed. In the twenty-first century politicians receive Muslim community concerns against Australia's role and involvement in the Middle East without inevitably reading into them any threat to national unity or other evidence of subversive conduct. But this is not due to an abandonment of reliance on the image of the subversive foreigner, but rather to the construction of Muslim and Arab communities in accordance with yet another image of the perpetual-foreigner-within. Far from having *overcome* the tendency to position non-British migrant communities as foreigner communities, from the 1970s with the transition to state multiculturalism, dominant white Australia has also progressively invoked a *third image* of the perpetual-foreigner-within, that of the 'submissive foreigner'.

Submissive foreigner communities are ethnic minority groups who respond positively when the state calls upon them perpetually to demonstrate their willingness to recognize the white Australian state's authority and the rightful belonging of its people. At the heart of the concept of the submissive foreigner is the view that the migrants' proper response to their perpetual foreigner position is not mere compliance with the demands and expectations of the white Australian authorities and people (as in the image of the compliant foreigner) but *submission to them with integrity*. With multiculturalism's institutional endorsement of the value of difference and cultural diversity, migrant and ethnic communities have been positioned in accordance with the logic underlying a *submissive foreigner* discourse.

Although new to the repertoire of the Anglophone foreigner discourses, the image of the submissive foreigner had been elaborated as a migrant community discourse as early as the period leading up to Federation. The 1897 formation of Australia's first Greek community association illustrates this. In the wake of the establishment of a newly federated *White Australia*, a handful of Melbourne's migrants from Greece gathered together to form their community organization, the *Greek Orthodox Community of Melbourne and Victoria*. The Community's founders were eager to maintain their distinctive cultural heritage in the British colony where they lived as foreigners and successful businessmen. Significantly, they saw no contradiction in their actions. From their perspective as submissive foreigners, absolute devotion to their own Greek national origins did not bar them from demonstrating genuine political allegiance to the Australian state or from showing respect for the presumed higher status of its British people as was expected of the foreigners. On the contrary, they took the view that to render public the precise nature of their dual loyalties was to supply evidence of a *moral character* and *integrity* in the foreigners that rendered them trustworthy and hence worthy of the British-Australian authorities' acceptance. As such migrant and ethnic community discourses reveal, the perpetual-foreigners-within are more than the epistemological constructions of dominant white Australia. They are indeed 'subjectivities formed simultaneously through privilege and oppression', who, as Damien Riggs, demonstrates in a different context, often in asserting their own claims to equal rights, nevertheless contribute to the ongoing dispossession of the Indigenous people.[72]

With the transformation of the submissive foreigner discourse from a migrant minority discourse to the framing logic of Anglophone official multicultural policy it became possible for community members to give their own definitions of ethnicity. For this reason the concept of ethnicity could no longer play the role of a racialized difference that *inevitably* marks migrant and ethnic communities as unassimilable outsiders. Because ethnic communities can no longer function as the visible sites of a racialized unassimilable difference, this role has now been assigned to Australia's refugee detention centres. Moreover, dominant white Australia has differentiated between some elements of ethnic difference that are received as the *acceptable cultural capital* of its *individual* owners and other elements that continue to be marked as potentially subversive. Thus the now familiar ways of Southern European Australians fall into the first category whereas Muslim religious practices fall into the second. Nevertheless, due to the disassociation of ethnicity with the images of the subversive/compliant foreigner in the (post-)multicultural era, individuals now enter into public-political life without *presumed* loyalties to any particular ethnic community. State multiculturalism has accordingly acquired a covert meaning via its implication in the onto-pathology of white Australia and the latter's reliance upon the perpetual-foreigners-within. Far from doing away with migrants' ascription of their perpetual-foreigner status, it reinforces the social positioning of specific ethnic minority groups as the perpetual-foreigners-within in accordance with the three images of the subversive, the compliant or the submissive.[73]

---

72. Damien W. Riggs, *Priscilla, (White) Queen of the Desert*, New York, Peter Lang Publishing, 2006, p. 2 and p. 72.

73. In addition to the papers already cited, further discussion of the

The combined effect of the operation of the three images of the perpetual-foreigner-within is that the members of migrant and ethnic communities remain *white*-non-white and *white*-not-white-enough even if this is not always rendered fully visible. Regardless of the obvious asymmetries of power amongst the members of white Australia's various non-white and not-white-enough migrant and ethnic communities, non-Indigenous Australians are equally complicit in perpetuating white race privilege. As Aileen Moreton-Robinson explains, from an Indigenous perspective the most basic distinction still remains that between the Indigenous peoples and the white Australians understood as 'the migrant colonizers'.[74] This is so, even though the distinction attributes whiteness to migrant groups, such as 'the Asians' or 'the Indians', who from a different perspective would fall into the racial category of non-whites.

---

historical impact of the three images of the perpetual-foreigner-within can be found in Toula Nicolacopoulos and George Vassilacopoulos, 'The Concept of the Foreigner and Refugee Rights', *Social Alternatives* vol.29, no.4, 2002, pp. 45-49; Toula Nicolacopoulos and George Vassilacopoulos, 'Greek-Australian ComNicolacopoulos, Toula and Vassilacopoulos, George, 'Greek-Australian Community Development: Diversity and Solidarity in Place of Loyalty', in Centre for Citizenship and Human Rights (ed.), *Community Development Human Rights and the Grassroots Conference Proceedings*, Melbourne, Deakin University, 2004, pp. 182-194.; Toula Nicolacopoulos and George Vassilacopoulos, 'On the Other Side of Xenophobia: Philoxenia as the Ground of Refugee Rights', *Australian Journal of Human Rights*, vol. 10, no. 1, 2004, pp. 63-77; Toula Nicolacopoulos and George Vassilacopoulos, *From Foreigner to Citizen: Greek Migrants and Social Change in White Australia, 1897-2000*, (Greek) Melbourne and Pireas, Eothinon Publications, 2004.

74. Aileen Moreton-Robinson, 'I Still Call Australia Home', p. 23.

13. THE IMPERATIVE OF THE INDIGENOUS - WHITE AUSTRALIAN ENCOUNTER

We have argued that Indigenous survival and resistance generates the demand that white Australians approach our history philosophically. In becoming philosophical it is not enough for us to remember and admit that to be white Australian is to be implicated in the violent dispossession of Indigenous peoples. It is not even enough for us to remember or admit to past injustices whose effects are still being suffered today. We need to make a deeper more reflective turn to the emptiness of our being.

Having actively whitened not just the Australian institutions, but our self-instituting gathering-we, we have decisively undermined our sovereignty. Our being has been emptied out and our sovereign emerging in the world has thus been reduced to an active *non-emerging*. Indeed, as white Australians we are best described as 'the non-emerging' in the sense of beings who lack presence. Being present essentially involves a meeting of wills as bearers of worlds who encounter one another's presentation as the very pre-condition of their own possibility. Such an encounter is an affirmative act of mutual respect. The act of presenting my being through the uttering of the 'we' affirms both the radical ontological equality of property-owning subjects and a no less radical hierarchy since what one owns the other does not. But due to our failure to affirm such hierarchical equality in our encounter with the Indigenous peoples, we have compromised our 'we,' the sovereign gathering out of which our nationhood and institutions spring, and we have resorted to calling upon the perpetual-foreigners-within to misrepresent the white Australian collective as a being with presence. For this reason non-Indigenous Australians are no more than the mutually misrecognizing foreigners.

In the absence of this reflective relationship to our being, the being of the occupier, white Australians continue to be implicated in a betrayal of thought, which is manifested by the willful denial of the violence that defines our relationship to Indigenous dispossession and which informs the collective criminal will of white Australia. Regrettably our onto-pathology denies us the opportunity to live out our freedom to enjoy the ontological integrity of presence, to live as the bearers of living memory and, hence, as the memory of the living that might frame historical facts with the very fact of history, once and for all. Our continued exposure to the Indigenous peoples' defiance against their dispossession confirms our loss of living memory in the ontological sense we have described. White Australians are thus entirely dependent upon the Indigenous peoples for some semblance of an association with living memory, for a kind of memory that combines vision with the presence of ontological integrity.

Reflecting upon our past then does not just call for recognition that historical injustices warrant remedies, whether symbolic or calling for the return of lands, compensation for losses and other forms of redistribution of wealth. In the circumstances it requires an unconditional surrender to the sovereign Indigenous being, as a precondition of everything else, including the possibility of our own emergence as sovereign beings. In order for white Australians to realize our potential to emerge as sovereign subjects we must redress the self-inflicted compromised nature of our property-owning subjectivity by (re)instituting our white gathering-we at the ontological level. This, in turn, means confronting the question 'where do you come from?' and receiving the answer that the defiant Indigenous Australians already offer us as a gift. In such a double act of erasing and embracing, we would at once erase our claim to rightful ownership of Australian territory and embrace Indigenous peoples' sovereignty as that which already embraces our being. Given that recognition of Indigenous peoples as property-owning subjects in their own right is the only form of recognition available to us, redressing our ontological condition demands of us a radical reversal of the forms of engagement of private property-owning subjects with their world. That is, it demands, not that we retain possession of our material world but that we detach from it in order, ultimately, to regain the lost integrity of our subjectivity. The circumstances of the onto-pathology of white Australian being call for this sort of radical response in order for white Australians to accept and announce the emptiness of our empty being. Naming our being as empty and thereby giving a truthful account of our origins is ultimately to take responsibility for ourselves and for our actions as a collective.

This is the process through which to gain presence. For white Australians then our surrender to the sovereign Indigenous peoples is indispensable to gaining presence, the presence that is the fundamental precondition for engaging with our world. Of course in order to achieve this we must have both the courage to reject the imperative of whiteness, the imperative to 'act as if the land were initially without owners', as well as the vision to respond to the ontological command that the current times direct to property-owning subjectivity, the call to 'be as a person and respect others as persons'.

Because the above mentioned double act of erasing-embracing is the fundamental pre-requisite for creating an ontological vision of integrity and, relatedly, for becoming philosophically historical, the creation of a vision of the future, the vision of re-gathering that might take us beyond the current practices of the white Australian collective criminal will, makes possible a return to our past. Indigenous sovereignty is the key to this return. For the past two centuries, but perhaps today more than ever, the Indigenous—white

Australian encounter holds out the possibility of a movement for white Australians from the present as emerging presence to the future as vision, and from the future as vision to the past as living memory of the fundamental *as such* rather than to history as the graveyard of facts. This is how the primary concern for a historiography and a politics that have become sufficiently philosophical can be inspired by the ontological conditions that already shape our being—living memory, presence, and vision. Only within such memory, which has the power to reveal to us the opening that history itself is at the present moment, do facts acquire their genuine truth-bearing force, and only within the unfolding of an anamnesis that has the strength to remember both the past and the future does presencing—'I am, we are'—become possible. This is why the (re)writing of Australian history in such visionary terms can only result from Indigenous sovereignty.

REFERENCES

Anderson, Ian, 'Black Bit, White Bit', in Michelle Grossman (ed.), *Blacklines: Contemporary Critical Writing by Indigenous Australians*, Melbourne, Melbourne University Press, 2003, pp. 43-51.

Arnold, John and Attwood, Bain (eds.), *Power, Knowledge and Aborigines*, Melbourne, La Trobe University Press in association with the National Centre for Australian Studies, Monash University, 1992.

Attwood, Bain, *The Making of the Aborigines*, Sydney, Allen & Unwin, 1989.

Attwood, Bain, *Telling the Truth about Aboriginal History*, Sydney, Allen & Unwin, 2005.

Birch, Tony, 'Nothing has Changed: The Making and Unmaking of Koorie Culture', in Michelle Grossman (ed.), *Blacklines: Contemporary Critical Writing by Indigenous Australians*, Melbourne, Melbourne University Press, 2003, pp. 145-158.

Birch, Tony, 'The Invisible Fire: Indigenous Sovereignty, History and Responsibility', in Aileen Moreton-Robinson (ed.), *Sovereign Subjects: Indigenous Sovereignty Matters*, NSW Australia, Allen and Unwin, 2007, pp. 105-117.

Brady, Wendy, 'That Sovereign Being: History Matters', in Aileen Moreton-Robinson (ed.), *Sovereign Subjects: Indigenous Sovereignty Matters*, NSW Australia, Allen and Unwin, 2007, pp. 140-154.

Bunda, Tracey, 'The Sovereign Aboriginal Woman', in Aileen

Moreton-Robinson (ed.), *Sovereign Subjects: Indigenous Sovereignty Matters*, NSW Australia, Allen and Unwin, 2007, pp. 75-85.

Deleuze, Gilles, *Nietzsche and Philosophy*, trans. Hugh Tomlinson, New York, Columbia University Press, 1983.

Dodson, Michael, 'The End in the Beginning: Re(de)fining Aboriginality', in Michelle Grossman (ed.), *Blacklines: Contemporary Critical Writing by Indigenous Australians*, Melbourne, Melbourne University Press, 2003, pp. 25-42.

Falk, Phillip and Martin, Gary, 'Misconstruing Indigenous Sovereignty: Maintaining the Fabric of Australian Law', in Aileen Moreton-Robinson (ed.), *Sovereign Subjects: Indigenous Sovereignty Matters*, NSW Australia, Allen and Unwin, 2007, pp. 33-46.

Foley, Gary, 'The Australian Labor Party and the Native Title Act', in Aileen Moreton-Robinson (ed.), *Sovereign Subjects: Indigenous Sovereignty Matters*, NSW Australia, Allen and Unwin, 2007, pp. 118-139.

Goldberg, David Theo, *The Racial State*, Malden MA and Oxford, Blackwell Publishers, 2002.

Goldberg, David Theo, 'Racial states' in David Theo Goldberg (ed.), *A Companion to Racial and Ethnic Studies*, Massachusetts and Oxford, Blackwell, 2002, pp. 233-258.

Goldberg, David Theo, *The Threat of Race: Reflections on Racial Neoliberalism*, Malden MA, Oxford and Carlton Victoria, Wiley-Blackwell, 2009.

Grossman, Michelle (ed.), *Blacklines: Contemporary Critical Writing by Indigenous Australians*, Melbourne, Melbourne University Press, 2003.

Haggis, Jane, 'Beyond Race and Whiteness? Reflections on the New Abolitionists and an Australian Critical Whiteness Studies', *borderlands e-journal*, 2004, www.borderlandsejournal.adelaide.edu.au/vol3no2_2004/haggis_beyond.htm

Harris, Cheryl I., 'Whiteness as Property', *Harvard Law*

Review, vol. 106, no. 8, 1993, pp. 1707-1791; *UCLA School of Law Research Paper*, no. 06-35, available at SSRN: http://ssrn.com/abstract=927850.

Hegel, G.W.F., *Philosophy of Right*, trans. T.M. Knox, Oxford, Oxford University Press, 1967.

Homer, *The Odyssey*, trans. Robert Fagles, New York, Penguin, 1996.

Langton, Marcia, 'Dominion and Dishonour: A Treaty between our Nations?', *Postcolonial Studies*, vol.4, no.1, pp. 13-26.

Larkin, Steve, 'Locating Indigenous Sovereignty: Race and Research in Indigenous Health Policy-making', in Aileen Moreton-Robinson (ed.), *Sovereign Subjects: Indigenous Sovereignty Matters*, NSW Australia, Allen and Unwin, 2007, pp. 168-178.

Lea, Tess, Kowal, Emma and Cowlishaw, Gillian (eds.), *Moving Anthropology: Critical Indigenous Studies*, Northern Territory, Australia, Charles Darwin University Press, 2006.

Locke, John, *Two Treatises of Government*, (1689), P. Laslett (ed.), Cambridge, Cambridge University Press, 1988.

Lloyd, Genevieve, 'No one's Land; Australia and the Philosophical Imagination', *Hypatia*, vol.15, no.2, 2000, pp. 26-39.

Marr, David, 'Is the Media Asleep?' in Robert Manne (ed.), *Do Not Disturb: Is the Media Failing Australia?*, Melbourne, Black Inc Agenda, 2005, pp. 216-230.

Moreton-Robinson, Aileen, 'I still Call Australia Home: Indigenous Belonging and Place in a White Postcolonising Society', in Sara Ahmed, Claudia Cataneda, Ann Marie Fortier and Mimi Shellyey (eds.), *Uprootings/Regroupings: Questions of Postcoloniality, Home and Place*, London and New York, Berg, 2003, pp. 23-40.

Moreton-Robinson, Aileen, 'Tiddas Talkin' Up to the White Woman: When Huggins et. al. Took on Bell' in Michelle Grossman (ed.), *Blacklines: Contemporary Critical Writing by Indigenous Australians*, Melbourne,

Melbourne University Press, 2003, pp. 66-77.

Moreton-Robinson, Aileen, 'Introduction: Resistance, Recovery and Revitalization' in Michelle Grossman (ed.), *Blacklines: Contemporary Critical Writing by Indigenous Australians*, Melbourne, Melbourne University Press, 2003, pp. 127-131.

Moreton-Robinson, Aileen, 'Whiteness, Epistemology and Indigenous Representation' in Aileen Moreton-Robinson (ed.), *Whitening Race: Essays in Social and Cultural Criticism*, Canberra, Aboriginal Studies Press, 2004, pp. 75-88.

Moreton-Robinson, Aileen, (ed.), *Whitening Race: Essays in Social and Cultural Criticism*, Canberra, Aboriginal Studies Press, 2004.

Moreton-Robinson, Aileen, 'How White Possession Moves: After the Word', in Tes Lea, Emma Kowal and Gillian Cowlishaw (eds.), *Moving Anthropology: Critical Indigenous Studies*, Northern Territory, Australia, Charles Darwin University Press, 2006, pp. 219-232.

Moreton-Robinson, Aileen, (ed.), *Sovereign Subjects: Indigenous Sovereignty Matters*, NSW Australia, Allen and Unwin, 2007.

Nicolacopoulos, Toula and Vassilacopoulos, George, 'The Concept of the Foreigner and Refugee Rights', *Social Alternatives* vol.29, no.4, 2002, pp. 45-49.

Nicolacopoulos, Toula and Vassilacopoulos, George, 'The Making of Greek-Australian Citizenship: From Heteronomous to Autonomous Political Communities', *Journal of Modern Greek Studies*, vol.11/12, 2003/4, pp. 165-176.

Nicolacopoulos, Toula and Vassilacopoulos, George, *From Foreigner to Citizen: Greek Migrants and Social Change in White Australia, 1897-2000*, (Greek) Melbourne and Pireas, Eothinon Publications, 2004.

Nicolacopoulos, Toula and Vassilacopoulos, George, 'Greek-Australian Community Development: Diversityand Solidarity in Place of Loyalty', in Centre for Citizenship and Human Rights (ed.), *Community Development*

Human Rights and the Grassroots Conference Proceedings, Melbourne, Deakin University, 2004, pp. 182-194.

Nicolacopoulos, Toula and Vassilacopoulos, George, 'Discursive Constructions of the Southern European Foreigner', in Ben Wadham and Suzanne Scheck (eds.), *Placing Race and Localising Whiteness Conference Proceedings,* Adelaide, Flinders University Press, 2004, pp. 73-81.

Nicolacopoulos, Toula and Vassilacopoulos, George, 'On the Other Side of Xenophobia: Philoxenia as the Ground of Refugee Rights', *Australian Journal of Human Rights*, vol. 10, no. 1, 2004, pp. 63-77.

Nicolacopoulos, Toula and Vassilacopoulos, George, 'Rethinking the Radical Potential of the Concept of Multiculturalism, in Tseen Khoo (ed.), *The Body Politic: Racialized Political Cultures in Australia (Refereed Proceedings from the UQ Australian Studies Centre Conference, Brisbane, 24-26 November 2004)*, Brisbane and Melbourne, University of Queensland Australian Studies Centre, and Monash University National Centre for Australian Studies, 2005.

Nicolacopoulos, Toula and Vassilacopoulos, George, 'Australian Multiculturalism: Beyond Management Models', in Reza Hasmath (ed.), *Managing Ethnic Diversity: Meanings and Practices from an International Perspective*, Surrey, Ashgate, 2011, pp. 141-176.

Nicolacopoulos, Toula and Vassilacopoulos, George, 'The Pulse of Chronos: Historical Time, the Eternal and Timelessness in the Platonic Gathering', *Parrhesia* vol.15, 2012, pp. 54-63.

Nicoll, Fiona, 'Reconciliation in and out of Perspective: White Knowing, Seeing, Curating and Being at Home in and against Indigenous Sovereignty', in Aileen Moreton-Robinson (ed.), *Whitening Race: Essays in Social and Cultural Criticism,* Canberra, Aboriginal Studies Press, 2004, pp. 17-31.

Nicoll, Fiona, 'De-facing *Terra Nullius* and Facing the Public Secret of Indigenous Sovereignty in Australia', *borderlands e-Journal*, vol.1, no.2, 2002, http://www.borderlands.net.au/vol1no2_2002/nicoll_defacing.html

Read, Peter, 'A Haunted land no Longer? Changing Relationships to a Spiritualised Australia', *Australian Book Review*, no. 265, 2004, pp. 29-34.

Reynolds, Henry, *Aboriginal Sovereignty*, Australia, Penguin Books, 1996.

'Special Issue on Indigenous Rights', *Australasian Journal of Philosophy*, vol.78, no.3, 2000.

Rigney, Lester-Irabinna, 'A First Perspective of Indigenous Australian Participation in Science: Framing Indigenous Research Towards Indigenous Australian Intellectual Sovereignty', *Kaurna Higher Education Journal*, vol.7, pp. 1-13.

Riggs, Damien W., *Priscilla, (White) Queen of the Desert*, New York, Peter Lang Publishing, 2006.

Stratton, Jon, *Uncertain Lives: Culture, Race and Neoliberalism in Australia*, Newcastle upon Tyne, UK, Cambridge Scholars Publishing, 2011.

Vassilacopoulos, George, 'Plato's *Republic* and the End of Philosophy', *Philosophical Inquiry*, vol. XIX, no.1-2, 2007, pp. 34-45.

Watson, Irene, 'Settled and Unsettled Spaces: Are We free to Roam?', in Aileen Moreton-Robinson (ed.), *Sovereign Subjects: Indigenous Sovereignty Matters*, NSW Australia, Allen and Unwin, 2007, pp. 15-32.

www.ingramcontent.com/pod-product-compliance
Lightning Source LLC
Chambersburg PA
CBHW030223170426
43194CB00007BA/838